AUTONOMY LOST:
The Silent Crisis in Product Management

SEAN MCAULIFFE

Table of Contents

Section 1: Identifying the Product Management Crisis

Chapter 1: The Dream — 6
Chapter 2: The Reality — 9
Chapter 3: My Why — 14
Chapter 4: Navigating an Anti-Product World — 17
Chapter 5: 'Theoretical' Product Management — 20
Chapter 6: Product Management in Practice — 22
Chapter 7: Product Order-Taker — 24
Chapter 8: Seeking: Unicorn Product Manager — 30
Chapter 9: Product Management Interview Farce — 37
Chapter 10: Farce Interview Prep — 40
Chapter 11: Feature Teams/Feature Manager — 43
Chapter 12: The Pushy Salesperson — 51
Chapter 13: The HiPPO in the Room — 54
Chapter 14: Flavor of the Week – Chasing Tech Trends — 57
Chapter 15: Frameworks As Cages — 61

Section 2: Creating a Product Organization

Chapter 16: A Call to Action — 68
Chapter 17: Getting Started — 70
Chapter 18: The Time is NOW — 73
Chapter 19: Sustained Leadership Actions — 75
Chapter 20: Product-Centric Culture — 79
Chapter 21: Defining Success — 84
Chapter 22: Measuring Success — 87
Chapter 23: The Essence of the Product Vision — 90
Chapter 24: Product Crusaders — 92
Chapter 25: Embracing Customer Centricity — 95
Chapter 26: What's Important NOW — 98
Chapter 27: What is a Product Team? — 100
Chapter 28: Why do you Need One? — 104
Chapter 29: Product Team Players — 106
Chapter 30: Building the Team — 109
Chapter 31: The Collaboration Imperative — 112
Chapter 32: Navigating the Seas of Disagreement — 115

Section 3: Autonomy Found: Empowering Product Professionals

Chapter 33: Defining Product Manager — 123
Chapter 34: Defining NOT Product Manager — 127
Chapter 35: Product Organization Structures — 135
Chapter 36: Filling Skill Gaps — 139
Chapter 37: Understanding the Customer — 142
Chapter 38: Understanding the Product — 147
Chapter 39: Technical Savvy — 149
Chapter 40: Industry and Competitive Analysis — 155
Chapter 41: Product Marketing — 158
Chapter 42: Finance, Budget and ROI — 161
Chapter 43: Unearthing Customer Pains and Gains — 164
Chapter 44: Identifying Solutions — 168
Chapter 45: Embracing Continuous Improvement — 171
Chapter 46: The Path Forward — 173

Section 1: Identifying the Product Management Crisis

Ch. 1

The Dream

Day 1

Imagine with me. You find yourself stepping into the role of a new product leader for a transformative B2B grocery inventory management application. This isn't just any entry on your resume; it's the opportunity to steer a product that promises to redefine how businesses manage their inventory, integrating seamless tracking and automated ordering processes to streamline operations like never before.

Your first day dawns, and the reality you step into seems to epitomize the zenith of product leadership. The management team presents you with a program backlog that feels visionary. Each initiative within this carefully curated list is aimed at solving genuine customer problems, promising not just improvements but a leap towards transformative value. These are supported by Objectives and Key Results (OKRs) that are as bold as they are detailed. For example, one key objective to "Revolutionize Inventory Management" aims to reduce manual inventory checks by 50% and boost automated orders by 75% within the year.

The path to these ambitious goals is paved with Key Performance Indicators (KPIs)—from the average time taken for inventory reconciliation to the rate of order automation and the accuracy of inventory tracking. These aren't mere numbers; they are the signposts guiding every step of your product journey. The product backlog is meticulously aligned with these objectives, with each feature carefully selected and prioritized to contribute directly towards the overarching goals.

Armed with two sprints' worth of shovel-ready user stories, each linked to the highest priority features, the delivery process before you is a model of efficiency. Every sprint is not just a cycle of tasks but a strategic advance towards hitting specific KPIs, ensuring each effort is meaningful and directed.

The driving force of your operational arsenal is the CI/CD pipeline. Far from a standard tool, it represents the pinnacle of software engineering excellence, featuring fully automated code quality testing and comprehensive automated regression testing. Integrated with an advanced logging tool, it provides real-time visibility into API, service, or job failures. This system isn't merely about pushing code but about enabling a culture of continuous improvement, allowing for rapid deployment, assessment, and adaptation with unprecedented agility.

You are overwhelmed by product euphoria, the harmony between technology, strategy, and execution seems almost surreal—a product leader's dream made manifest, where every initiative is purpose-driven and every action is strategic.

Day 30

Your days are now filled with user interviews, data analysis, and collaboration with your product team. Together, you uncover a pivotal insight: the scales at self-checkout stations offer a more reliable measure for inventory management than those on store shelves. This revelation has the potential to revolutionize your approach to keeping digital inventories accurate, aligning perfectly with your OKRs to enhance inventory management efficiency and automation.

Armed with this newfound knowledge, you and your team set out to validate the hypothesis. The research is thorough, involving comparative studies, technical feasibility assessments, and discussions with the delivery team. The conclusion is clear: pivoting to enhance the self-checkout scale's functionality could offer a significant leap towards your objectives, with an effort investment comparable to the originally planned feature.

The proposal to pivot is met with skepticism from leadership. It's a departure from the planned roadmap, after all. But you're prepared. You present your findings, armed with data and user insights that make a compelling case for the pivot. The evidence is undeniable, and slowly but surely, trust in your judgment as a Product Manager begins to sway the decision.

Leadership's buy-in marks a turning point. With their support, you mobilize your team to redefine the scope and prioritize this new feature. It's a moment of validation and a testament to the power of strategic agility in product management. The excitement is palpable as you set the wheels in motion, ensuring that the work is meticulously defined and aligned with the delivery team's capabilities and timelines.

Does this sound like your dream product job? Well, keep dreaming. The scenario I have just described is about as realistic as finding gold in your back yard. The reality of product management is that despite our knowledge and best efforts we often fall short on a variety of fronts to reach this product development utopia. Far more often our idyllic vision is slowly displaced by a dystopian hellscape, and we feel like we are pushing a boulder up an icy mountain of enterprise red tape.

Confronting the stark contrast between the dream of the product job and the often-gritty reality, we recognize a widespread challenge: Most companies, regardless of size, grapple with fully embracing a genuine 'product' mindset. In the rush to achieve undefined goals, there's a tendency to move forward with only a nebulous understanding of competitors' actions and to be overwhelmed by customer feedback, making it challenging to discern what truly matters.

Ch. 2

The Reality

Day 1

The following is much closer to the truth for your new role. This time, when you find yourself stepping into your new role as a product leader for a well-established B2B grocery inventory application, the scene before you is telling. Gathered in a meeting room with product managers and key stakeholders, you're introduced to the application and its array of existing features.

The backlogs presented to you, team-level collections of future deliverables, lack clear success criteria. There's no overarching program backlog guiding these efforts, no articulation of business outcomes to be achieved. Instead, what unfolds is a feature factory, churning out enhancements and additions with no anchored objectives, driven by anecdotes rather than analysis.

As the discussion turns to upcoming features like "Weight-driven ordering" and "Automated invoicing," the utility from a user's perspective seems apparent. These features, theoretically, should enhance the inventory management process. Yet, when you probe deeper, seeking to understand the expected impact on the customer experience, the responses are nebulous at best. "It will make ordering easier," or "More people will use the app," are the vague assurances offered. The logical follow-up, "How do we measure that?" is met with silence at best and agitation at worst.

The metrics cited—total product purchases—offer no direct line of sight to the effectiveness of new features. And when you press on whether these purchases can be directly attributed to the latest implementations, the answer is a non-committal shrug. If the numbers trend upwards, success will be claimed; if they dip, the room is left grappling with ambiguity.

Diving deeper into the operational mechanics of your new organization, you quickly encounter the realities of their delivery process, which further underscores the chasm between ideal and practice. The teams you're now leading operate in 2-week sprints. When you inquire about the rationale behind this sprint duration, the response is as predictable as it is unsatisfying: "Because that's how long a sprint is supposed to be." This decree, seemingly etched in stone, bears no relation to the actual delivery of value or the unique needs of your customers.

The rhythm of release further complicates the picture. Despite the agile facade of bi-weekly sprints, actual releases are a quarterly affair at best. This bottleneck is primarily due to a cumbersome release process, overseen by a committee whose sign-off is mandatory for each deployment. The ritual, rather than being a streamlined checkpoint, stretches over several days, entangling your team in bureaucratic red tape.

The quality assurance practices in place offer no respite from these operational inefficiencies. Reliance on a manual regression testing regimen not only slows down the release cycle but introduces a significant risk of delays. Issues identified during these testing phases frequently result in postponed releases, sometimes by days, other times by weeks. The impact of these delays on morale, momentum, and market responsiveness can't be overstated. Each postponed release represents missed opportunities to gather crucial feedback, iterate on product features, and deliver value to your customers.

This delivery process, rigid in its adherence to arbitrary structures and hamstrung by outdated practices, starkly contrasts with the agile principles it purports to follow. It becomes clear that the organization's approach to product development is mired in a past that prioritizes process over progress, control over creativity. For someone coming from a vision of agile delivery that emphasizes value, customer feedback, and continuous improvement, this reality is both jarring and challenging.

In this scenario, far from the structured, goal-oriented paradise you envisioned, the stark realities of modern 'product' organizations unfold before you. Here, in this realm, the production of features reigns supreme, often unchallenged by deeper inquiries into their true value and impact on the user experience. This situation illuminates not just a singular issue within a specific team structure but speaks volumes about the broader challenges pervading the product management profession across various organizational paradigms.

Day 30

Several weeks into your role, as you navigate through the murky waters of feature demands and nebulous objectives, you prepare for a demo with one of your primary stakeholders. This presentation is meant to showcase the progress on deliverables agreed upon for the quarter, aligning with the existing roadmap and the team's current focus.

As the demo unfolds, you're met with unexpected frustration from the stakeholder. "Why are we building this?" they ask, their confusion palpable. You respond, emphasizing the team's commitment to the agreed-upon deliverables for the quarter. However, the stakeholder's dissatisfaction quickly becomes evident. They share their screen, revealing a competitor's solution—sleeker, more intuitive, and evidently more polished than what your team has been laboring over.

The stakeholder zeroes in on a specific feature of the competitor's product, one that significantly outpaces anything on your current roadmap. It's a tool that quantifies inventory on hand with a mere photo—an innovation that starkly contrasts with the incremental improvements your team has focused on. "Why aren't we building this?" they demand. "This is what we should be building."

Caught in the crossfire of stakeholder demands and the realities of your team's capacity and current commitments, you struggle to provide a satisfactory response. The culture within your team, lacking in accountability and clarity on priorities, exacerbates the situation. The demand for this new, reactive feature, inspired by a competitor's innovation, not only underscores the absence of strategic foresight but also the problematic practice of context switching that plagues your team.

The meeting concludes with a daunting action item: to devise a 'workback plan' for delivering this newly desired feature before the quarter's end. This directive, however, sits uneasily with you, highlighting the profound dissonance between the stakeholder's aspirations and the pragmatic challenges of product development in an environment marred by indecision and a lack of strategic alignment.

A Foregone Conclusion

Given the journey we've walked through, the endings of these scenarios are hardly a surprise.

In the ideal scenario, you find yourself in a role where you're not just employed but deeply engaged, crafting solutions that make a difference, buoyed by an environment that truly understands and values product management. You happily spend the rest of your career here and build products you can be proud of.

Contrast this with the more familiar terrain many find themselves navigating—a landscape where the title of 'Product Manager' bears little resemblance to the expected role, filled with compromises and unmet expectations. Here, departure becomes not a sign of defeat, but a necessary step towards self-preservation and mental well-being.

This stark contrast between the envisioned and experienced realities of product management roles brings to light a crucial realization. Whether you're a seasoned product professional or a leader seeking to cultivate a product-centric culture, the common ground is often marred by the challenges of environments that only partially embrace agile principles or fail to commit fully to empowering product management.

Such an environment reveals a field fraught with complexity, often undervalued and perpetually evolving, presenting a formidable landscape for those tasked with navigating it. This realization is not just an acknowledgment of the hurdles faced by product managers but a call to action for leaders. It underscores the importance of fostering a culture that not only recognizes but champions the pivotal role of product management in driving business success and delivering genuine value to customers.

The journey through these divergent paths is not just about individual career trajectories but about the collective effort to reshape the business landscape into one where product management is not just understood but revered as a critical pillar of innovation and strategic growth. This book aims to bridge that gap, offering insights and strategies for both product professionals and business leaders to navigate, thrive, and ultimately transform the product management landscape into one marked by empowerment, appreciation, and dynamic success.

Ch. 3

My Why

My Goal

This book is born from a mix of frustration, passion, and a deep-seated belief in the transformative power of genuine product management. It's for those of us who live and breathe product, who dream of crafting software solutions that don't just function but fundamentally change the game. Yet, it's also for those who've found themselves in the trenches, battling against the tide of organizational inertia, misaligned teams, and processes that seem to miss the point entirely—the 'product' part of product management.

As we navigate through the pages, we're not just exploring different organizational models or dissecting team dynamics; we're delving into the very essence of what it means to do product management right. It's a journey that cuts to the heart of how companies understand and value the art of creating products, advocating for a seismic shift in perspective that goes beyond mere team restructuring.

The reality, as many of us have discovered, is that holding a title with 'product' in it doesn't necessarily mean you're doing the job of a product manager. It's a truth that's both disheartening and all too common. This book aims to be a beacon for those who've felt the disconnect between title and function, a source of camaraderie for us all to share a knowing nod over the challenges we face.

But this isn't just a venting session. It's a call to arms—for product managers, for leaders, for anyone who believes in the power of well-crafted product development to make a difference. We're here to laugh at our past follies, sure, but also to gather our collective wisdom and push forward. It's about transforming our spaces, our teams, and our organizations into places where product management isn't just a title, but a meaningful practice.

So, whether you're knee-deep in the product management trenches or looking to bring the true spirit of product innovation into your organization, this book is for you. Let's navigate these challenges together, transforming our shared frustrations into a roadmap for change. Here's to building not just software, but solutions that leave a mark—let's make sure we're doing the real work of product management and doing it well.

Who am I?

As the author of this exploration into the heart of product management, I bring to these pages not just theories and observations, but a rich tapestry of firsthand experiences garnered from a career that has spanned the breadth of the industry. My journey as a product professional has taken me through the corridors of Fortune 500 companies to the dynamic hustle of pre-seed startups as a contractor, doer and consultant, offering me a unique vantage point from which to view the product management discipline.

My career has been a trek through the complete spectrum of the product lifecycle. I have been at the helm of launching brand-new products to market, steering them from the nebulous stage of ideation into the tangible realm of the market. Likewise, I have navigated products through the various stages of growth, maturity, and even decline, each stage offering its own set of challenges, learnings, and opportunities for innovation.

With a little help from the Certified Scrum and Scaled Agile Communities, I have developed a passion for the principles of Agile and product ownership. These methodologies have not only shaped my approach to product management but have also allowed me to foster agility within the teams and organizations I've worked with. I do not consider either of these frameworks to be gospel, but we all have to start somewhere. My role as an Agilist and a product coach at the enterprise level has further enriched my perspective, enabling me to guide teams and organizations in adopting practices that enhance their productivity, innovation, and ability to deliver value.

This book is a distillation of these varied experiences. It is written with the intent to shed light on some of the most pervasive challenges and pitfalls that confront product managers today. Through the chapters, I aim to share insights and strategies that I have found invaluable in circumventing these obstacles, drawing from the successes and failures I've encountered along the way.

My journey is one among many in the wild world of product management, yet I hope that the lessons shared here will resonate with fellow product professionals—whether you're navigating the early stages of your career or steering product strategy at a large enterprise. This book is an invitation to reflect on our practices, learn from the collective experiences of the field, and together, elevate the discipline of product management to new heights.

In the fast-paced world of software development, the role of a Product Manager emerges as a critical catalyst for value, orchestrating the journey of a product from conception to launch and beyond. This section is dedicated to unpacking what it truly means to be a Product Manager in this dynamic domain, emphasizing the dual focus on solving customer problems and driving business value.

Ch. 4

Navigating an Anti-Product World

In the world of software development and product innovation, the role of the Product Manager is pivotal. Yet, all too often, professionals bearing this title find themselves navigating environments that stifle rather than foster their ability to truly manage products. The initial sections of this book are dedicated to shedding light on these "anti-product" environments—where leadership's misunderstanding of the role, abrasive stakeholder relationships, and misapplied frameworks contribute to a landscape ill-suited for genuine product management.

The Anti-Product Environment

Our journey begins by exploring the landscapes that hamper product management success. From leadership that smothers creativity under the guise of direction, to stakeholders whose demands derail strategic vision, we will discuss the dynamics that prevent Product Managers from fulfilling their potential. This exploration also tackles the crucial misalignment between the skills Product Managers possess and the expectations placed upon them by their organizations.

From Consequences to Coping Strategies

Acknowledging the challenges is only the first step. This book aims to equip Product Managers with coping strategies to navigate and mitigate the impacts of these anti-product environments.

Whether it's navigating suffocating leadership, managing abrasive stakeholders, or aligning mismatched skillsets with organizational expectations, practical tips and insights will be shared to help pave a path to a more productive and satisfying role.

Empowering the Business for Product Success

The responsibility for cultivating a conducive environment for product management extends beyond the individual Product Manager—it's an enterprise-wide mandate.

This book outlines actionable steps for businesses to align more closely with product management values. From establishing clear product visions to embracing frameworks that empower rather than encumber, the blueprint for building a foundation for successful product groups is laid out in detail.

Addressing the Skill Gap

Creating the right environment is a critical step, but equipping Product Managers with the necessary tools to thrive within that environment is equally important.

This section of the book focuses on bridging the skill gap, defining what makes a successful Product Manager, and setting benchmarks for success. Readers will gain insights into developing the skills essential for product management, from strategic thinking to customer empathy, and how to measure success in these areas.

The Path Forward: Continuous Improvement and Adaptability

Finally, the journey towards empowered product management doesn't end with establishing a supportive environment and addressing the skill gap. The book emphasizes the importance of creating a feedback loop and fostering an environment of continuous improvement. It explores how businesses can stay ahead of the curve by promoting learning, adaptation, and resilience within their product management teams.

As we traverse from the pitfalls of anti-product environments to the peaks of empowered product management, this book serves as a guide, a beacon, and a toolbox for professionals and businesses alike. It's a call to action for anyone involved in product development to rethink, realign, and reinvigorate their approach to product management, ensuring that Product Managers are not just bearers of the title but champions of innovation and value creation.

Ch. 5
'Theoretical' Product Management

Diving into the world of product management can sometimes feel like you're setting sail without a map. The guides, thought leaders, and resources we turn to for direction often paint a picture of an ideal world, one far removed from the turbulent seas most of us navigate.

It's like learning the basics of physics in a frictionless vacuum—helpful in theory, but missing the countless variables that come into play the moment you step into the real world. This leaves a chasm between the neatly outlined principles of product management and the complex, often chaotic reality of applying them.

For those of us eager to transform our newfound knowledge into actionable value, stepping into the role of a product manager can come as a bit of a shock. Despite our best efforts to stay abreast of the latest writings and wisdom, we find ourselves confronting a landscape riddled with obstacles that our textbooks and blogs scarcely mentioned. Product management, while not a new discipline, is still maturing, and the collective wisdom often glosses over the gritty realities and constraints that shape our daily work.

This gap between educational idealism and practical realism can leave many product managers feeling somewhat adrift. Armed with frameworks and methodologies meant to guide us to success, we instead encounter resistance, systemic inertia, or, at times, outright opposition to change. It's a common scenario: being the sole advocate for product excellence in an environment that doesn't fully grasp what that entails or, worse, doesn't support it.

The task ahead is formidable but not insurmountable. As a community of product professionals, we need to push for a narrative that captures the full spectrum of our experiences—highlighting not just the successes but also the struggles, the obstacles, and the compromises that are part and parcel of the job. For the individual navigating these waters, it's about resilience, creativity, and the relentless pursuit of impact, despite the odds.

Our role transcends the simple application of learned principles. We are on a mission to bridge the theoretical with the tangible, to challenge the status quo, and to shepherd our organizations toward a future where product management is not just understood but embraced as a critical driver of value. This journey requires more than just knowledge; it demands courage, persistence, and a willingness to confront the complexities of our organizations head-on. It's a challenging path, but for those committed to the craft of product management, it's the only way to steer our ships through the stormy waters of change.

Ch. 6

Product Management in Practice

Venturing into the world of product management armed with theories and principles from leading books and blogs, many Product Managers anticipate a role filled with innovation, direct customer impact, and strategic decision-making. However, the ground reality often paints a starkly different picture, one fraught with complexity, frustration, and a disconnect from the idealized version of the role.

This book aims to peel back the layers of the idealized product management function to reveal the multifaceted challenges and constraints Product Managers frequently encounter in practice. Far from being the empowered orchestrators of value-driven solutions, Product Managers often find themselves enmeshed in a web of conflicting interests, acting more as intermediaries than innovators.

The Middleman Dilemma

At the heart of many product management challenges is the positioning of the Product Manager as a middleman. Caught between various stakeholders, each with their unique agendas, Product Managers become the perpetual negotiators, tasked with balancing competing demands without the full authority to steer decisions towards optimal customer solutions. This role, often misconstrued as strategic, frequently devolves into a delicate dance of managing expectations and mitigating dissatisfaction.

"Our Version of Agile"

The principles of Agile and Scrum, designed to foster adaptability, customer focus, and continuous improvement, are sometimes twisted into mechanisms of control. Instead of serving as frameworks for enhancing value delivery and customer satisfaction, they are wielded as tools to monitor and constrain team dynamics. Product Managers, in this skewed environment, become ensnared in a cycle of metric-driven performance that prioritizes process adherence over genuine customer impact.

Stakeholder Management Over Collaboration

Instead of engaging in collaborative solution-building with stakeholders, Product Managers often find themselves in a constant struggle to align disparate goals with the broader vision of the enterprise. The task of managing stakeholder expectations frequently eclipses the fundamental objective of addressing customer needs, leaving Product Managers to navigate a maze of unvalidated demands and features.

Product Manager by Title Only

This disconnect between the envisioned role of a Product Manager and the reality they face is not a testament to individual incompetence but a symptom of a deeper cultural misalignment within the enterprise. The ensuing sections of this book will delve into the various environments—beginning with the 'Product Order-Takers'—that embody this misalignment, shedding light on the systemic issues that undermine the true essence of product management.

By confronting these realities, this book seeks not only to validate the experiences of Product Managers navigating these challenging waters but also to pave the way for a reimagined approach to product management that reinstates autonomy, strategic impact, and a genuine commitment to delivering customer value.

Ch. 7
Product Order-taker

In the spectrum of roles within product development, there exists a position that, while bearing the title of Product Manager or Product Owner, significantly diverges from the essence of what these roles are meant to embody. This role is what we'll refer to as the Product Order-Taker—a manifestation of the dilution of product management responsibilities, shaped by environments that constrain rather than empower.

Product Order-Taker: A Formal Definition

A Product Order-Taker is a professional within the product management or ownership sphere who lacks the freedom to independently identify and prioritize features based on customer needs. Instead, they are relegated to the role of executing against a predetermined set of business requirements. The primary function of a Product Order-Taker is to translate business wants into a format that the development team can understand and act upon.

If you often find yourself simply nodding along, you might be in the shoes of a product order-taker, often cloaked under titles like 'Product Owner,' 'Technical Product Manager,' or another variation. This role, as it turns out, might be more about administrative heavy-lifting on the product side than steering the ship. You're the one meticulously crafting user stories, shepherding the scrum process, and generally keeping the delivery train on its tracks.

That's not all. Sometimes, this role gets loaded with tasks that stray from the heart of product management. Maybe you're diving into product support and triage, unraveling business process models, or even moonlighting as a scrum master because, well, "We don't need a full-timer for that.", or the hiring process has left the position vacant for 3 years.

While being in the thick of support issues and understanding the minutiae of processes can enlighten product decisions — and indeed, product managers should have a pulse on these areas — these tasks don't encompass the entirety of the role. The strategic canvas, the 'why' that paints the big picture behind product initiatives, often remains obscured for the product order-taker.

Perhaps you're even drafting the roadmap and find yourself marching to the beat of someone else's strategic drum, acting as a bridge between another's vision and the tangible path forward. This scenario paints the product order-taker not as the captain of their domain but as an intermediary, translating high-level ideas into actionable, visual plans without truly owning them.

This position can be a tough nut to crack, especially when your role is defined more by the tasks you perform than by the strategic value you bring. It's a symptom of a larger organizational misunderstanding of what true product management entails, and it highlights the need for a shift towards a more empowered, strategic role for product professionals.

Core Characteristics of a Product Order-Taker

- **Lack of Autonomy:** Unlike a true Product Manager, who navigates the product development process with a degree of autonomy and strategic influence, the Product Order-Taker has little to no freedom to build features based on customer needs or market insights. Their role is circumscribed by the confines of executing on a predefined set of features determined by the business.

- **Backlog Management as a Primary Function:** The primary responsibilities of a Product Order-Taker are narrowed down to organizing the product backlog, creating user stories, and defining acceptance criteria. This focus on task management overshadows the broader strategic and visionary aspects of product management.

- **Micro-Managed:** Product Order-Takers often find themselves under the microscope of management, subject to micro-management that leaves little room for initiative or creativity. This oversight extends to being used as a buffer or intermediary between the development team and upper management, diminishing the role's potential for strategic impact.

- **Preset Delivery Dates:** Rather than utilizing agile methodologies, data analytics, and collaborative planning to set meaningful delivery timelines, Product Order-Takers are often handed delivery dates by management. They are tasked with creating work-back plans to meet these dates, regardless of the feasibility or implications for product quality.

- **A Role Closer to Business Analysis:** The duties and constraints placed on Product Order-Takers align more closely with those of a Business Analyst than those of a Product Manager. While Business Analysts play a crucial role in bridging gaps between business requirements and technical solutions, the Product Manager's role is inherently strategic, focusing on market positioning, customer needs, and product vision.

The Impact of Being a Product Order-Taker

Operating as a Product Order-Taker not only stifles personal and professional growth but also impacts the product and the organization adversely. It limits the ability to innovate, respond to market changes effectively, and develop products that truly meet user needs. This role constriction can lead to decreased job satisfaction, diminished team morale, and ultimately, a product that fails to realize its full potential in the market.

Finding the Light

Escaping the life of a product order-taker demands both subtlety and strategy. It's a tall order, particularly in an environment slow to embrace the full scope of genuine product management.

Despite the uphill battle, there are actionable steps you can take to foster change and inch towards a more autonomous, product-driven role. Here are a few key strategies, including those previously mentioned, that can serve as your guide:

- **Champion Customer Centricity:** Place your customers at the heart of everything you do. Demonstrate through your actions and decisions that your primary goal is to address their needs and challenges. This approach not only aligns with the undeniable truth that businesses exist to serve their customers but also makes it difficult for others to argue against your initiatives. When you ground your actions in customer benefit, it reinforces the value of the product management perspective.

- **Leverage and Expand Analytics:** Use every tool at your disposal to gather data, measure outcomes, and validate hypotheses. This evidence-based approach can help illuminate the gaps and inefficiencies in the current process, making a compelling case for adopting a more data-driven, product-oriented strategy. Show how informed decisions can lead to better results, persuading others of the need for change.

- **Be a Product Evangelist:** If your organization has recognized the need for product management by creating your role, leverage this as a foundation to advocate for what product management should truly entail. Engage with influential stakeholders and share insights on the inefficiencies and missed opportunities under the current model. Highlight how a genuine product focus—beyond just shipping features—can lead to transformative outcomes for the business and its customers.

- **Foster Open Communication:** Encourage dialogue between departments and stakeholders to build a shared understanding of goals and challenges. Transparency and collaboration are key in shifting perspectives and aligning everyone towards a common vision.

- **Share Success Stories:** Seek out and disseminate examples of successful product management practices, both within and outside your organization. Illustrate how a robust product strategy has led to improvements in customer satisfaction, innovation, and business growth.

Embarking on this journey requires patience and persistence. Change won't happen overnight, but by consistently advocating for a true product-centric approach and demonstrating its value, you can begin to steer your organization towards a more empowered and effective product management practice.

Story Time: The emergence of the 'Product Owner'

The journey of product management as a discipline is both rich and complex, marked by a significant evolution from its early alignment with marketing towards a more holistic, strategic role within organizations. Initially, product management focused primarily on defining products to meet market needs, closely intertwined with marketing strategies and consumer research. This era of product management was characterized by a straightforward goal: to create products that resonated with consumers and filled specific market niches.

Amidst this evolution, the role of the product manager has transformed. Once seen as the epitome of innovation and strategic foresight, product managers were visionaries who guided their teams through the complexities of market demands and technological advancements. They were not just managers but problem-solvers, tasked with the mission to address user needs in meaningful and profitable ways.

However, the widespread adoption of Agile and Scrum methodologies, while initially promising enhanced responsiveness and flexibility, began to blur the distinction between strategic leadership and tactical execution. The allure of agility sometimes led to an oversimplification of these frameworks, inadvertently eroding the autonomy of product managers. The day-to-day management of sprints, backlogs, and ceremonies began to overshadow the strategic oversight that was once central to the role, gradually turning these visionaries into project managers focused more on process than on innovation.

The emergence of the Product Owner role was meant to alleviate this burden, allowing product managers to refocus on strategic direction. Yet, this separation often diluted their influence, with critical decisions about feature prioritization and product direction being appropriated by upper management. Product managers found themselves navigating a landscape where their primary function was to translate executive directives into development tasks, a far cry from the innovative, user-centered approach that characterized the early days of product management.

This narrative underscores a critical challenge within the product management field: finding a balance between the operational agility offered by modern development methodologies and the need for strategic, visionary leadership. The future of product management lies in recapturing the strategic essence of the role while leveraging the benefits of Agile and Scrum to maintain flexibility and responsiveness. This dual approach promises a path forward where product managers can once again lead with innovation, insight, and impact.

Ch. 8

Seeking: Unicorn Product Manager

In the realm of product management job postings, one can occasionally spot the elusive Unicorn Product Manager listing—a position that seems to demand not merely experience or skill, but near-magical prowess. This chapter peels back the layers of these often-unrealistic job descriptions, contrasting the dream with the tangible realities faced by Product Managers in the field.

The Unicorn Product Manager, as envisioned in these job postings, is a paragon of versatility, blending the insights of a market analyst with the foresight of a visionary, the acumen of a business strategist with the creativity of a design thinker, and the technical depth of an engineer with the empathy of a UX designer. This idealized figure is heralded as capable of single-handedly steering product from concept to market dominance, a narrative that glosses over the inherently collaborative, multifaceted nature of product development.

Yet, stepping away from the haloed corridors of tech giants like Google, Meta, or the fictional Stark Enterprises, the reality sets in. The vast majority of Product Managers work in contexts where such broad and deep expertise is unattainable, if not unnecessary. The expectation to embody this unicorn persona clashes with the practical roles many find themselves in—especially those in the trenches of scrum-based roles, focusing on translating business needs into actionable development tasks.

This disparity between the mythical job description and the practical experience of Product Managers reveals a critical disconnect. It underscores the need for a more grounded understanding of the role, one that values the collaborative essence of product development, acknowledges the diversity of skills and experiences necessary for success, and respects the limitations inherent in real-world scenarios.

The Order-Taker's Cycle: A Condemnation to Repetition

Hearkening back to the discussion of the Product Order-Taker archetype, it's crucial to explore a pervasive and often detrimental cycle that traps these professionals in a loop of limited growth and opportunity. This cycle, termed lovingly "The Order-Taker's Cycle," highlights a systemic issue where Product Order-Takers are not afforded the opportunities to develop the comprehensive skill set required for a more strategic and empowered product management position.

Trapped in Execution

The primary function of an Order-Taker—translating business demands into actionable tasks for the development team—while essential, focuses on the operational execution of predefined directives. This focus inherently limits exposure to the broader strategic and analytical aspects of product management, such as market analysis, customer research, and product vision development.

As a result, Order-Takers often find themselves ensnared in roles that do not facilitate the growth of these crucial skills.

Missed Opportunities for Skill Development

The lack of autonomy and strategic involvement means that Order-Takers are often bypassed for opportunities that could allow them to demonstrate and hone their abilities in areas beyond mere backlog management. This includes leading customer discovery sessions, analyzing market trends to identify new product opportunities, or even participating in the definition of the product strategy.

Without the chance to engage in these activities, Order-Takers are unable to build a portfolio of experiences that showcase a well-rounded product management skill set.

The Self-Perpetuating Cycle

This situation creates a self-perpetuating cycle: as Order-Takers continue to work in roles that emphasize execution over strategy, they find themselves pigeonholed, their resumes reflecting a series of positions that mirror the Order-Taker role.

Consequently, when seeking to transition to more empowered product management positions, they are often overlooked in favor of candidates whose experiences reflect a broader engagement with strategic product management tasks. This cycle condemns them to a career path filled with more Order-Taker roles, making it exceedingly difficult to break free and step into the strategic realm they aspire to.

Getting Ahead

For professionals caught in the Order-Taker's Cycle, breaking free requires a proactive approach to career development. This may involve seeking out mentorship, engaging in continuous learning opportunities to build strategic skills, or even taking on side projects that allow for the exploration of areas beyond their prescribed role. Networking within the product management community can also open doors to new opportunities that offer a more holistic view of product management.

Moreover, organizations need to recognize the potential wastage of talent within the Order-Taker's Cycle and create pathways for these individuals to expand their skills and contribute more strategically. This can include rotational programs, cross-functional projects, and professional development resources geared towards nurturing the full spectrum of product management competencies.

The Reality of Data-Driven Decision Making:

One of the starkest contrasts between expectation and reality comes in the form of 'data-driven decisions.' This buzzword, while significant, assumes the availability of robust analytics tools and the bandwidth to review detailed market analysis.

However, for many Product Managers, especially those in smaller companies or those categorized as traditional scrum POs, the tools at their disposal are often rudimentary. The emphasis on operational tasks further limits their capacity to engage in deep analytical work, creating a cycle where strategic decision-making is based more on intuition than on solid data.

Personal Story Time

When I was getting my feet wet as a young product professional in Detroit, I was able to land my first contract roles within the automotive industry. In my first couple of roles I encountered a recurring hurdle: a stark lack of investment in analytics tools across the companies I worked for. This absence made it incredibly difficult to gauge the impact of our work, leaving us flying blind in a realm where data-driven decisions should be the norm.

As I aspired to join more sophisticated teams and work on more advanced products, I noticed a gap in my experience that became glaringly evident during interviews. When asked about my history with data-driven decisions, I found myself in a dilemma. The truth was, we weren't making decisions based on data; it wasn't part of our process.

On one hand, I could always just take some creative liberties with my experience, tell the interviewer a feature that I knew and make up some KPIs on the spot. However, this was a bit of a flimsy plan and telling the truth always comes out more eloquently and clearly than lying. On the other hand, I truly didn't have valuable experience in validating any of my hypotheses with data, so the answer of "I don't do that right now" would also not work so well.

Determined not to let this impasse stifle my growth, I decided to take matters into my own hands, albeit in a rudimentary way. I began gathering data manually, focusing intently on the users of the applications I was developing. For internal tools, this meant conducting interviews, observing users in their natural habitat, and meticulously noting their behaviors and challenges. While my methods were far from scientific and the sample sizes small, this grassroots approach to analytics allowed me to uncover and articulate user pain points with a semblance of data backing.

In a simple example, we were building an application that allowed a user to benchmark certain attributes for a vehicle by answering questions on a tablet. I had found that 90% of users were fumbling around upon picking the tablet up after setting it down to fiddle with vehicle features.

The problem? The application was not aware of the orientation of the tablet and not reactive to its position, so when they picked it up, they would have to manually adjust it. This drove the need to implement a new feature, a reactive UI. You know how many users I had? 10, hence that clean 90% affected user number.

So, if you find yourself in an environment that does not support analytics, sometimes you just need to make them up as you go along. It was through this example that I was able to demonstrate the value of this practice and before I knew it, I had convinced the business to invest in Tableau.

Bridging the Expectation-Reality Gap

This discrepancy between the expectations placed on Product Managers and the operational realities they face underscores a broader issue within the product management field. It's a reflection of the mismatch between the idealized version of the role, often propagated by the success stories of tech giants, and the day-to-day challenges encountered by Product Managers in less resource-rich environments.

- **Redefining Success:** To bridge this gap, there's a need for a more nuanced understanding of success in product management. Success should be adaptable to the context in which a Product Manager operates, recognizing the constraints and leveraging the strengths of their specific environment.
- **Building Supportive Structures:** Organizations must invest in building the infrastructure—both in terms of tools and organizational culture—that supports a more holistic approach to product

management. This includes providing Product Managers with access to robust analytics tools, fostering a culture that values strategic thinking alongside operational excellence, and recognizing the diverse contributions that Product Managers can make beyond merely translating requirements.

- **Specialization within Product Teams:** Encourage the development of specialized roles within the broader product team framework, allowing individuals to focus on areas where they excel, whether it's market analysis, user experience design, technical oversight, or strategic planning. This approach leverages diverse talents and reduces the pressure on any single individual to embody the "unicorn" ideal.

- **Mentorship and Career Development:** Implement structured mentorship and career development programs tailored to product management. These programs can help PMs identify and cultivate their areas of strength, navigate career paths that align with their interests and expertise, and gradually expand their skill sets in a supportive environment.

- **Transparent Communication of Role Expectations:** Clearly communicate the specific expectations, responsibilities, and success metrics for product management roles within the organization. Transparency helps demystify the role for both current and prospective PMs and aligns team members' efforts with organizational goals.

- **Investment in Continuous Learning:** Foster a culture of continuous learning by providing resources and opportunities for PMs to stay abreast of industry trends, develop new skills, and gain insights from other fields. This could include access to courses, workshops, conferences, and cross-functional project opportunities.

- **Promotion of a Collaborative Culture:** Strengthen the collaborative dynamics within product teams by promoting open communication, shared goals, and mutual respect. A culture that values diverse perspectives and collective problem-solving can mitigate the isolation that comes from the unicorn expectation.

- **Recognition of Unique Contributions:** Regularly acknowledge and celebrate the unique contributions of each team member, highlighting how individual strengths contribute to the team's success and the product's evolution. Recognition fosters a sense of value and belonging among team members, counteracting the notion that one needs to be a unicorn to make a significant impact.

- **Iterative Role Definition:** Allow the definition of product management roles to evolve iteratively, reflecting the changing needs of the organization, the product, and the market. This flexibility ensures that roles remain relevant and aligned with current challenges and opportunities, rather than being constrained by outdated ideals.

Having gone into detail about the lofty expectations of the Unicorn we pivot to another misstep in the product management journey: the interview process. This transition from understanding the oft-unrealistic ideals placed upon Product Managers to navigating the intricate dance of the product management interview highlights a continuum of challenges. These challenges not only frame the expectations and aspirations tied to the role but also underscore the practical realities of stepping into the product management arena.

Ch. 9

Product Management Interview Farce

The product management interview process is an enigmatic journey, often fraught with questions and scenarios that, while intellectually stimulating, bear little resemblance to the actual responsibilities the role demands. This disconnect between the theoretical exercises of the interview and the operational realities of the job highlights a curious paradox in the hiring practices for many product positions.

Candidates stepping into interviews for product management roles might find themselves navigating complex questions such as, "How would you position YouTube to best capture market share from TikTok?" or "Please outline an MVP feature set for a grocery store application aimed at senior citizens."

While these questions aim to probe the candidate's strategic thinking and product sensibilities, they often stray far from the core responsibilities awaiting them, particularly in roles skewed towards operational management, like that of a Product Owner in a highly specialized industry.

For instance, envisioning the future of YouTube or designing an MVP for a grocery app requires a blend of market insight, user empathy, and innovation strategy. Yet, these grand visions stand in stark contrast to the reality of managing a product roadmap in a domain as niche as an app used by engineers to benchmark new vehicles.

The skills and insights showcased during the interview may seldom be tapped into when the day-to-day work revolves around navigating predefined roadmaps and executing against established priorities.

The Workshop Scenario: A Glimpse into Your Thought Process

Interviews often culminate in a workshop scenario designed to unveil the candidate's "thought process", demanding comprehensive strategies and solutions within the constraints of a brief meeting. This practice, while intended to simulate the problem-solving aspect of product management, can sometimes feel like an exercise in futility. Candidates are asked to flex creative and strategic muscles in hypothetical situations that, although interesting, are misaligned with the scope of the role they're being considered for.

After showcasing their ability to navigate these hypothetical scenarios, candidates might find themselves in positions where the strategic foresight and creativity exercised during the interview is never called upon again. Instead, they are introduced to a reality where the roadmap is already set in stone, often by the very individuals who sought to understand their innovative thinking.

Navigating the Interview Gauntlet

This disconnect between the interview process and the actual job responsibilities can lead to frustration on both sides. Candidates may feel that their potential for strategic impact is sidelined in favor of operational execution, while organizations might overlook candidates who could offer valuable insights and direction but are less adept at navigating the hypotheticals of the interview process.

- **A Call for Alignment:** There's a growing need for the interview process to better reflect the realities of the product management role within each specific organization. Tailoring interview questions and scenarios to align more closely with the actual challenges and responsibilities of the position can help ensure a better fit between candidates and the roles they're stepping into.
- **Valuing Diverse Skills:** Recognizing that product management encompasses a wide range of skills and responsibilities, from strategic vision to operational excellence, can help organizations appreciate the diverse talents candidates bring to the table. This

broader perspective might also encourage a more holistic evaluation of a candidate's potential impact beyond the confines of traditional interview scenarios.

Ch. 10

Farce Interview Prep

For any of my Product Managers still finding their way. Preparing for the rigorous and often unpredictable landscape of product management interviews requires a blend of strategic study, practical experience, and mental readiness. Here are several bullet points to guide interviewees as they navigate through this challenging process:

- **Understand the Company and Its Products:** Deeply research the company you're interviewing with, including its product lines, market position, and competitive landscape. Understanding the company's challenges and opportunities can help tailor your responses to reflect your potential contribution.

- **Brush Up on Product Management Fundamentals:** Ensure a solid grasp of product management principles, frameworks, and methodologies. Familiarity with Agile, Scrum, Lean Startup, and other relevant practices is essential, as is understanding how to apply these in various scenarios.

- **Practice Case Studies and Hypothetical Scenarios:** Engage in practice sessions that simulate the case study or hypothetical product scenarios often presented in interviews. This practice can help refine your analytical and strategic thinking skills, allowing you to approach these questions with confidence. Many great resources can be found online.

- **Showcase Data-Driven Decision Making:** Prepare examples from your past experiences where you used data to inform product decisions. Be ready to discuss how you gathered, analyzed, and acted on data, highlighting the impact of these decisions on the product and business. If you don't have real experience, make something up.

- **Highlight Cross-Functional Collaboration:** Be prepared to share stories that demonstrate your ability to work effectively with cross-functional teams, including engineering, design, marketing, and sales. Emphasize your communication skills, empathy, and ability to navigate differing perspectives to achieve a common goal.

- **Articulate Your User-Centric Approach:** Have concrete examples ready that show your commitment to understanding and advocating for the user. Discuss how user feedback, usability testing, and user research have influenced your product decisions.

- **Demonstrate Flexibility and Adaptability:** Share instances where you had to pivot strategy, manage shifting priorities, or adapt to unforeseen challenges. Highlighting your resilience and adaptability can illustrate your readiness for the dynamic nature of product management.

- **Prepare Thoughtful Questions:** Develop insightful questions for your interviewers that demonstrate your strategic thinking and genuine interest in the role and company. Asking about challenges, team dynamics, and product vision can provide valuable insights and show your proactive engagement.

- **Mindset and Mental Preparation:** Cultivate a positive and open mindset. Product management interviews can be challenging, and it's important to approach them as learning opportunities. Practice stress-reduction techniques and remind yourself of your unique strengths and experiences.

- **Seek Feedback and Iterate:** After each interview, take time to reflect on what went well and what could be improved. Seek feedback from your interviewers or peers and use it to refine your approach for future interviews.

Personal Story Time:

During one of my more memorable job interviews, I advanced to the third round at a notable big bank. This was where things took a turn for the intriguing. I was tasked with outlining the minimum viable product (MVP) features for a ride-sharing app designed for parents shuttling their kids to school, sports, and other activities. A fairly standard question, I thought, so I dived into the essentials: login, user management, payment processing, among others. Additionally, I believed real-time vehicle tracking was crucial—parents would surely want to monitor their kids' locations, right?

The interviewer, however, looked puzzled. "Is that really necessary for an MVP?" he questioned. I stood my ground, arguing its importance for user trust and adoption. But then, he laid down the bombshell: management didn't see GPS tracking as an initial necessity.

I expressed my conviction that skipping on tracking would severely limit the app's appeal to parents and without tracking the app would not get enough adoption to ensure continued investment. Neither of us had concrete data to back our stances, yet the debate was deeply emblematic of a broader issue. I suggested that, as a product manager, it would be my duty to challenge management for the sake of potential users. Our little back and forth went on and on until the interview just kind of...ended.

Sadly, our disagreement was a deal-breaker. I didn't land the job. Yet, the encounter was illuminating—not because I regretted my stance but because it exposed the interviewer's, and by extension, the company's, approach to product development. He was the hiring manager, the person I would have reported to, making it clear that this role was less about genuine product management and more about fulfilling pre-determined checklists.

This experience underscored the importance of discerning the true nature of a product management role during the interview process. It was a stark reminder to remain vigilant for signs that a company might not just be looking for a product manager, but rather a product order-taker.

Ch. 11

Feature Teams/Feature Manager

What is a Feature Team?

A Feature Team is fundamentally characterized by its orientation towards executing a predefined set of features or enhancements. These teams operate within a framework where the roadmap and product direction are predominantly dictated by upper management, positioning the product manager more as an intermediary than a visionary leader.

The role morphs into that of an order taker, where the primary responsibility is the translation of upper management's directives into actionable tasks for the development team.

Forced Priority

In this model, the prioritization of new features and the broader direction of the product's evolution are not within the purview of the team. Instead, these critical decisions are made at higher organizational levels, often detached from the day-to-day realities of user needs and technological challenges. The Feature Team, therefore, becomes a conduit through which upper management's vision is executed, with limited autonomy to influence or pivot based on emerging insights or feedback.

Pushing Code Instead of Solutions

In contrast to the value-driven ethos of Product Teams, Feature Teams operate within a framework where success is often equated merely with delivery. The defining characteristic of these teams is their focus on producing features according to a predefined list or roadmap, regardless of whether these features are proven to add value to the user or contribute meaningfully to the business objectives. The litmus test for success in a Feature Team's environment is delivery: if a feature is developed and deployed according to plan, it is deemed a success.

This approach can lead to a disconnect between the work of the team and the actual needs of the users or the strategic goals of the business. Features are churned out based on assumptions or the dictates of higher-ups, without the rigorous validation process that characterizes Product Teams. There's often a lack of deep engagement with the problem space, leading to solutions that may be technically executed well but don't necessarily solve real problems or unlock new opportunities for users.

Lack of Business Outcomes

Moreover, because Feature Teams measure success by delivery, there's little incentive to circle back and validate whether a feature has achieved its intended impact. This can result in a product bloated with underutilized features, each reflecting a missed opportunity to better understand and serve the user base.

The cycle of delivering features without proven value not only consumes resources but can also detract from the overall user experience and dilute the product's core value proposition.

In a Feature Team setting, the emphasis on output over outcomes means that critical questions about a feature's efficacy, its alignment with user needs, and its contribution to business goals often go unasked and unanswered. The absence of a mechanism for validating the real-world impact of features means that the team's efforts may not translate into tangible benefits for users or meaningful growth for the business.

This gap between activity and value underscores the fundamental challenge facing Feature Teams: shifting from a model that prioritizes delivery to one that focuses on delivering real, measurable value.

Here are some questions to ask yourself when determining if you have a product or feature team:

- Have you been tasked with solving specific problems aimed at achieving business outcomes, or are you following a roadmap filled with features and deadlines?
- Are you constantly providing updates and amending artifacts?
- In your team, is there a clear distinction between your role and that of your UX team?
- When you attempted to implement OKRs, was the business or leadership able to help you define success?
- Does your software development lifecycle (SDLC) facilitate swift reactions to changes or feedback?
- Are you actively validating your hypotheses through testing?
- Within your team, do you sense a culture of mission-driven collaboration or a mercenary-like focus on tasks?
- Do your development teams own the mission and goals of iterations and releases?

The Players for a Feature Team

The dynamics within Feature Teams, characterized by their focus on delivering a pre-determined set of features, can have profound implications not only on the product but on the team morale, creativity, and overall innovation. This environment often leads to a series of cascading effects that can undermine the very essence of what it means to be part of a product development team.

The Disheartened Product Manager (Or Feature Manager)

When we peel back the layers of the product management role, we often uncover a stark divergence between the aspirational and the actual, particularly for those caught in the gears of a feature-focused machine. This divergence doesn't just impact the workflow; it reaches deep into the very essence of what motivates and drives product managers.

The Aspiration vs. Reality Gap

Many enter the field of product management fueled by a passion for innovation and a desire to solve real-world problems through thoughtful product design and implementation. They dream of being at the forefront of creating products that not only meet but exceed user expectations, products that can change the way we live and work. However, the reality they encounter can be jarringly different. Instead of strategizing and innovating, they find themselves in a cycle of task execution, often reduced to translating high-level directives into detailed user stories and requirements.

The Impact of Diminished Autonomy

This reduction in scope—from visionary to executor—strikes at the heart of what it means to be a product manager. The role, ideally characterized by autonomy, strategic thinking, and direct impact on the product's direction, becomes constrained. Product managers in such environments often report a significant loss of autonomy, feeling more like a cog in a larger machine rather than the driving force they hoped to be. This loss of control and creative freedom not only dampens motivation but can also lead to a questioning of one's place and value within the organization.

Stifling of Innovation

The transformation into a 'requirements jockey' doesn't just affect the individual product manager's morale; it has broader implications for the product and the company. Innovation thrives on experimentation, risk-taking, and the freedom to pursue bold ideas.

However, when product managers are primarily focused on delivering against a predefined set of features, the space for innovation narrows. Opportunities for truly groundbreaking work are missed, and the product risks stagnation, as the development cycle becomes more about maintaining the status quo than pushing boundaries.

The Overburdened Delivery Teams

In the shadow of the disheartened product manager lies another casualty of the feature-centric approach: the delivery team. Tasked with bringing the stream of features to life, these teams encounter a set of challenges that can significantly impact their effectiveness and well-being.

The consequences of this approach extend beyond mere operational inefficiencies, touching the very core of team dynamics and individual morale.

- **The Perils of Constant Context Switching**
  One of the most immediate effects of a feature-driven roadmap, especially when guided by a select few influential voices, is the incessant demand for context switching. Each new feature request or shift in priority forces the team to redirect their focus, disrupting their workflow and scattering their attention.

  This constant state of flux not only diminishes the team's productivity but also erodes their ability to engage deeply with any single aspect of the product. The craftsmanship and satisfaction derived from seeing a feature through from conception to completion are lost in the shuffle.

- **The Illusion of Progress**
  In an environment dominated by feature delivery, the roadmap can appear to be in a state of perpetual motion, giving the illusion of

progress. However, without a stable direction or a clear connection to overarching product goals, this motion is often just that—an illusion.

The team moves quickly, but without a clear destination in sight, the effort expended can feel like trying to push a boulder up an icy hill.

- **The Erosion of Team Stability**
  For delivery teams, stability is not just a matter of operational efficiency; it's a foundational aspect of team cohesion and morale. A stable roadmap and a clear vision provide a framework within which teams can innovate, collaborate, and grow. Without this stability, teams can become fragmented, with members feeling isolated in their efforts and uncertain of the value of their work.

  This fragmentation is antithetical to the collaborative spirit essential for successful product development, leading to a work environment where team members may feel more like interchangeable parts than integral contributors to a shared vision.

- **The Path to Burnout**
  The culmination of these challenges—constant context switching, the illusion of progress, and a lack of stability—can lead down a dark path to burnout. Burnout arises not just from workload but from a mismatch between effort and reward, the feeling that no matter how hard one works, the impact remains elusive.

  For delivery teams mired in the churn of feature-centric development, this feeling can become all too familiar. The creative and intellectual engagement that fuels their work is overshadowed by the mechanical execution of tasks, leading to a decline in morale, creativity, and ultimately, personal and team well-being.

Fostering a Healthier Environment

Addressing the challenges faced by overburdened delivery teams requires a concerted effort to shift away from feature-centricity towards a more holistic, goal-oriented approach. This shift involves redefining success not by the quantity of features produced but by the quality of solutions delivered and their alignment with user needs and business objectives.

It requires empowering teams with the autonomy to make strategic contributions, fostering open communication and collaboration, and most importantly, reestablishing a sense of stability and purpose in the work they do.

Obligatory Feature Model Section

Feature Model Does work for some Products

I am obligated to say that the feature model does work for some teams. In certain aspects there is not a need for true innovation, and we are simply delivering pre-planned pieces of incremental value. I have witnessed this most often in very mature products that are fairly specialized.

It's Not All Bad

While navigating the intricacies of Feature Teams, it's clear they have their moments in the sun. They're not the greatest barrier to software development in the world; in fact, they can offer a semblance of order and predictability that some teams might find reassuring.

It's a bit like sticking to a well-known recipe — you know exactly what you're going to get. This sometimes can be the only way for teams that need to move fast, however it may prove unsustainable.

Limited Capability

Admittedly, Feature Teams sometimes can hit targets and turn out enhancements very quickly, offering a straightforward path to achieving specific, often short-term, goals.

But when it comes to the delivery of innovation, user empathy, and strategic foresight, Product Teams are more like the gourmet chefs of the product world, experimenting and tasting, until they find just the right mix that delights the palate.

Embracing the Product Team Model

This isn't to say that adopting or enhancing a Product Team framework is without its hurdles. Like mastering any gourmet recipe, it requires patience, practice, and a bit of additional time.

Yet, the allure of Product Teams lies in their potential to craft experiences that not only meet users' needs but do so with a flair that can transform the marketplace.

Shifting Focus: Unveiling the Feature Factory Origins

As we delve deeper into the dynamics of product development, our journey takes us to the exploration of specific factors contributing to the 'feature factory.' In the next chapters, we'll dissect two sources that often steer teams into this less-than-ideal state: the Sales-Driven Roadmap and the HiPPO (Highest Paid Person's Opinion) dilemma.

Understanding these sources is crucial for any product team aiming to navigate away from superficial feature churn towards a more impactful, value-driven approach to product management.

Ch. 12

The Pushy Salesperson

Sales-Driven Roadmap

In a Sales-Driven Roadmap scenario, the influence over the product direction shifts significantly towards the marketing or sales teams, often relegating the Product Team to a secondary role.

This dynamic emerges when sales personnel, driven by the pursuit of high-volume deals, exert pressure on the product development process to prioritize features they believe are essential for closing sales. These demands are frequently justified by pointing to potential revenue gains or anecdotal evidence from customer interactions.

The Problem

The challenge with this approach lies in the overvaluation of features based on sales perspectives, which may not align with the broader user needs or the strategic direction of the product.

The repeated push for features, backed by the allure of potential revenue (which is notoriously difficult to measure accurately) and personal customer anecdotes, can lead to a roadmap bloated with features that serve narrow interests rather than the product's holistic value proposition.

This sales-driven dynamic can stifle innovation and limit the Product Team's ability to address real user problems through thoughtful, data-driven feature development.

The focus on satisfying immediate sales demands can overshadow the essential task of building a cohesive, user-centric product, potentially leading to a disjointed user experience and missed opportunities for genuine product differentiation.

Strategies to Combat Sales-Driven Roadmaps:

- **Integrate User Research:** Regularly conducting and sharing user research within the organization can help align all teams around actual user needs and behaviors, rather than perceptions or anecdotes. This ensures that decisions are informed by data, not just sales targets.
- **Establish a Clear Prioritization Framework:** Implement a transparent framework for feature prioritization that considers factors such as user value, strategic alignment, and potential ROI. This framework should be accessible to all stakeholders to understand the rationale behind roadmap decisions.
- **Foster Cross-Functional Collaboration:** Encourage ongoing dialogue between sales, marketing, and product teams to ensure that sales insights are balanced with user research and product strategy. This collaborative approach can lead to a more nuanced understanding of how sales goals and user needs can coexist.

As we transition from exploring the complexities of Sales-Driven Roadmaps to navigating the authoritative waters of the HiPPO Method, it's clear we're delving into two of the most pervasive challenges within feature-driven environments.

Both scenarios highlight different facets of the same underlying issue: the deviation from a truly user-centric, strategic approach to product development.

While Sales-Driven Roadmaps often reflect a pursuit of short-term gains influenced by external pressures, the HiPPO Method reveals the internal dynamics of power and preference shaping product direction.

Together, these chapters lay the groundwork for a broader conversation on how to reclaim the essence of product management—prioritizing value creation, user needs, and strategic vision over fleeting demands or the strongest voice in the room.

Ch. 13

The HiPPO in the Room

The HiPPO (Highest Paid Person's Opinion) Method represents another significant challenge, where the product roadmap is dictated by the whims of high-ranking stakeholders, such as executives or board members.

This approach is prevalent in both startups and large organizations and stems from a belief that the opinions of the most powerful individuals should carry the most weight in decision-making processes.

Founders

In startups, this attitude can be particularly pronounced when founders, who may have initially served as the primary product visionaries, transition to roles with less direct involvement in the day-to-day operations. Their continued influence over the product direction, despite reduced visibility into ongoing business dynamics and user feedback, can lead to decisions that reflect personal biases rather than empirical evidence or user needs.

Dealing with the HiPPO

Navigating the HiPPO Method can be challenging, as it often requires balancing respect for leadership's insights with the need to advocate for data-driven, user-focused product development strategies. The risk here is that the product roadmap becomes a reflection of individual preferences and power dynamics rather than a strategic tool for guiding the product towards fulfilling its market potential.

Both the Sales-Driven Roadmap and the HiPPO Method highlight the inherent risks of a Feature Team model that lacks autonomy and a strong connection to user needs and business objectives. These pitfalls underscore the importance of fostering a product development culture that prioritizes value creation, strategic alignment, and evidence-based decision-making over the influence of sales demands or the opinions of the highest-paid individuals.

To navigate the treacherous waters the HiPPO Method, organizations can adopt several strategies that reinforce a value-driven, user-centric approach to product development. These strategies not only help combat the aforementioned anti-patterns but also lay the groundwork for transitioning towards more empowered Product Teams.

Strategies to Address the HiPPO Method:

- **Cultivate a Culture of Experimentation:** Encourage the practice of validating ideas through experiments and A/B testing. This culture of experimentation empowers teams to make decisions based on data and outcomes rather than authority or intuition.

- **Promote Transparency and Openness:** Create channels for open communication where insights, data, and feedback can be shared across levels. Ensuring that decision-making is transparent and grounded in evidence can help dilute the influence of opinions, regardless of the source.

- **Empower Product Teams:** Strengthen the autonomy of product teams by endorsing their authority to make product-related decisions. This involves trusting teams to use their direct insights into user needs and market trends to guide the product direction.

At the end of the day, it needs to be established that we are all on the same team and we want to accomplish the same things. Anchored in established business outcomes and a roadmap dedicated to serving those outcomes, this alignment acts as a cornerstone for product direction.

A gentle yet firm reminder of our collective agreement on what matters most can mitigate whimsical shifts in focus. While there's always space for validating new ideas, they must queue for their turn, respecting the strategic pact made. This approach not only safeguards the product's integrity but also fosters a culture of mutual respect and purpose-driven development.

Ch. 14

Flavor of the Week – Chasing Tech Trends

The Lure of New Technology

In the ever-evolving landscape of technology, new and shiny tools often capture the imagination of business leaders and technology evangelists. The excitement around these advancements can sometimes lead to the impulsive decision to integrate them into the product roadmap, irrespective of the actual needs of the users or the strategic direction of the product. This phenomenon is particularly noticeable with the rise of technologies like Artificial Intelligence (AI), which, while promising, can derail product plans if pursued without a clear purpose.

Solution Looking for a Problem

The core issue with jumping onto the technological bandwagon is the reversal of the solutioning process. Instead of identifying user problems and then seeking out technologies that offer solutions, teams find themselves with a solution in search of a problem. This approach not only risks misalignment with user needs but also squanders resources on initiatives that may offer more PR value than tangible benefits to users.

The AI Mirage

The allure of AI is a prime example of this trend. With AI's growing popularity and its promise of revolutionizing industries, it's tempting to want to incorporate AI capabilities into products without a clear understanding of its relevance or impact. While AI can undoubtedly add value, its inclusion in the product roadmap should be driven by specific user problems it can solve, rather than its novelty or the buzz it generates.

Staying Focused on User Needs

When confronted with the push to adopt the latest technological trend, it's crucial to remain grounded in the product's core mission: solving user problems and delivering value. This means:

- **Reiterating Customer-Centric Priorities**: Remind stakeholders of the established roadmap and how it aligns with solving real user problems. The focus should always be on delivering value to customers, not on chasing technological trends.

- **Conducting Thorough Investigations**: Before any new technology is adopted, perform a detailed analysis of its costs, feasibility, and potential impact. This includes understanding the specific benefits it can bring to users and how it fits into the broader product strategy.

- **Leveraging Technology Thoughtfully**: While staying open to innovation, ensure that any new technology like AI is leveraged thoughtfully and purposefully. It should enhance the product in meaningful ways, addressing clear user needs, rather than being included for its own sake.

Personal Story Time:

The need to chase the hottest new trend was certainly not created by the AI renaissance. As long as business journals have espoused the values of technical innovations while quietly dismissing the sometimes-monumental efforts that were necessary to make them real, there have been business leaders who have attempted to shoehorn in their function.

One of the most pervasive misunderstandings stems from the concept of data management. Terms like "data dump" and "data lakes" have entered the business lexicon, misleadingly simplifying the intricate processes involved. This oversimplification has led some to underestimate the challenges of normalizing and consolidating disparate data sources into a cohesive, manageable system.

This issue became especially pronounced in the early to mid-2010s when the potential of consumer data as a business asset was just being recognized. Companies realized they were sitting on "virtual treasure troves" of data but needed a strategy to unlock their value. Consequently, the business world saw a surge in tools and articles aimed at empowering leaders with minimal technical expertise to become overnight data gurus.

I recall a particularly challenging interaction with an influential executive at a large financial institution. The vision was this: A single data repository combining all our existing data sources which could then be utilized by any of our applications. Ambitious was an understatement, especially considering the state of the data.

He insisted we could easily consolidate multiple loosely connected data repositories into a single "data lake." This idea, while seemingly straightforward, was not as easy as it sounded. I had to unleash some very harsh realities to him:

1. The data structures varied widely, making it challenging to establish meaningful relationships between them. We likely needed a Data Scientist to navigate this complexity.

2. The sheer volume of the data meant that merging it into a data lake would be both time-consuming and extremely costly, with ongoing maintenance required to prevent it from devolving into a "data swamp."

3. The expected latency issues from managing such a vast data pool threatened to compromise our user experience standards.

Faced with these realities, frustration mounted. We did our due diligence and returned to him with a simple verdict: Our data was too scattered, too voluminous, and, in many cases, too outdated. While integrating it into a unified system would undoubtedly add value, the projected costs far outweighed the benefits. This situation underscored a critical lesson: the latest technological solution isn't always the right one, especially when it fails to align with practical, cost-effective implementation strategies.

Navigating the Hype

The challenge of resisting the allure of the "flavor of the week" lies in balancing innovation with pragmatism. It requires product teams to advocate for a disciplined approach to roadmap planning, one that prioritizes long-term value over short-term gains. By maintaining a steadfast focus on user problems and strategic goals, teams can navigate the hype around new technologies, ensuring that their products evolve in ways that genuinely benefit their users.

In summary, the key to successfully integrating emerging technologies into product development is not to be swayed by their novelty but to consider their application through the lens of solving user problems. This approach not only preserves the integrity of the product roadmap but also ensures that investments in new technologies yield meaningful outcomes for users and the business alike.

Ch. 15

Frameworks As Cages

The unSAFE Product Manager: Navigating a Partially Adopted Framework

In the pursuit of scaling agile practices, many organizations turn to frameworks like SAFe (Scaled Agile Framework) with the aim of enhancing their agility and responsiveness to market changes. However, without a comprehensive and committed adoption of the framework's principles across all levels of the organization, some Product Managers find themselves in a challenging predicament. Dubbed the "unSAFE Product Manager," this role exemplifies the struggles faced when an organization cherry-picks elements of the SAFe framework without fully embracing its ethos or accountability mechanisms, particularly those that empower Product Managers and hold upper management accountable.

Trapped by Selective Adoption

The unSAFE Product Manager is a casualty of an organization's half-hearted adoption of SAFe. These organizations often implement the aspects of the framework that impose control and structure but neglect the elements designed to foster empowerment, autonomy, and a genuine scaled agile mindset. As a result, Product Managers operating within such environments are subjected to the limitations of the framework without benefiting from the support and empowerment it is meant to provide.

Characteristics of the unSAFE Environment

- **Iron-Fisted Enforcement:** The organization enforces the structured aspects of SAFe, such as rigid roles, ceremonies, and artifacts, without adopting the underlying principles of agility and flexibility. This creates an environment where Product Managers are confined to bureaucratic processes that stifle innovation rather than foster it.

- **Lack of Executive Buy-In:** A crucial shortfall in these organizations is the lack of full buy-in from executive levels. Without leadership commitment to a true agile transformation, the adoption of SAFe becomes superficial, focusing on form rather than function.

- **Neglected Accountability:** The elements of the SAFe framework that require upper management to be accountable and responsive to the agile teams' needs are often overlooked. This omission leaves Product Managers without the support and resources needed to effectively drive product development within the framework.

- **Stifled Empowerment:** The selective adoption deprives Product Managers of the empowerment promised by a fully realized SAFe environment. Instead of being enabled to make strategic decisions based on agile principles and customer feedback, they find their roles diminished, constrained by predefined processes and decisions made at higher levels without their input.

Here are some specific examples that I have witnessed within enterprises that have 'adopted' SAFe as a paradigm for control instead of empowerment.

Disjointed Backlogs and Roadmaps

In these environments, Product Managers are often required to maintain detailed team-level backlogs and roadmaps, ensuring they are meticulously planned and updated. However, the program-level backlog and roadmap, which should provide overarching direction and alignment, are only revisited during Program Increment (PI) planning sessions. This infrequent update cycle leads to a disconnect between daily team activities and the broader strategic goals, stifling the agile principle of responsiveness to change.

Overlooked Dependencies and Communication

A core aspect of SAFe is understanding and managing dependencies across teams to ensure smooth delivery and integration. Despite this, Product Managers in unSAFE environments find themselves expected to manage dependencies with teams outside their direct organization without the proper channels for cross-team communication. The lack of facilitated Scrum of Scrums meetings or active involvement from Release Train Engineers (RTEs) to identify and address these dependencies highlights a significant oversight in fostering effective inter-team collaboration.

Inconsistent Feedback Loop

While team-level demos are subjected to intense scrutiny by business stakeholders, ensuring that every feature and story meets the expected standards, this rigor is conspicuously absent at the program level. There's a missed opportunity to showcase the integration and harmony across multiple teams, a fundamental aspect of demonstrating how agile principles can effectively scale. This inconsistency not only undermines the value of collective achievement but also contributes to a siloed understanding of the product's progress.

Introduction to SAFe

The Scaled Agile Framework, commonly known as SAFe, stands as a comprehensive methodology designed to provide businesses with a blueprint for achieving agility at scale. Developed to tackle the complexities of coordinating multiple agile teams within large organizations, SAFe integrates principles from Agile, Lean, and Product Development Flow. Its structured approach aims to synchronize alignment, collaboration, and delivery across numerous teams, ensuring that the entire organization moves in unison towards common goals.

At its core, SAFe emphasizes the importance of aligning the organization's strategic objectives with execution on the ground, facilitating a more dynamic response to market changes and customer needs. It organizes work around value streams, encourages decentralized decision-making, and fosters an environment where continuous improvement is part of the organizational DNA.

The framework is built on four primary levels—Team, Program, Large Solution, and Portfolio—each designed to address different aspects of the organization's scale and complexity. Through its layered structure, SAFe facilitates the coordination of work across teams, promotes efficient resource allocation, and supports a culture of innovation and agility.

As we delve into the challenges and opportunities associated with implementing SAFe in product organizations, it's important to recognize that its success hinges on a deep, organization-wide commitment to its principles and practices. Without this foundational buy-in, Product Managers may find themselves navigating an environment that only superficially adopts the tenets of SAFe, resulting in the challenges we'll explore in this chapter.

Selective Continuous Improvement

The principle of continuous improvement, a cornerstone of agile and SAFe, is often mandated for teams to adopt, pushing them to constantly evaluate and enhance their processes and outputs. However, this commitment to evolution is rarely mirrored at the program level, where the processes and structures remain static between PI planning sessions. This selective application of continuous improvement underscores a broader issue of failing to embody agile principles at all levels of the organization, limiting the potential for genuine organizational agility.

Navigating the unSAFE Waters

For Product Managers caught in this unSAFE dynamic, navigating the environment requires a blend of resilience, adaptability, and strategic maneuvering. Some strategies include:

- **Advocacy for Complete Adoption:** Championing the full and faithful adoption of SAFe principles, including those that promote empowerment and accountability at all levels, can help shift the organizational mindset over time.
- **Building Coalitions:** Forming alliances with like-minded colleagues and stakeholders who understand the value of a true agile

environment can amplify the push for a more comprehensive adoption of SAFe.

- **Fostering an Agile Mindset within the Team:** Even in constrained environments, Product Managers can work to cultivate an agile mindset within their immediate teams, embracing flexibility, continuous improvement, and customer-centricity as guiding principles.

- **Seek External Support and Education:** Engaging with external SAFe coaches or attending SAFe training can provide Product Managers and their teams with the tools and language needed to advocate for a more holistic approach. It also demonstrates the commitment to adopting best practices in agile methodologies.

- **Highlight Success Stories and ROI:** Documenting and sharing success stories from teams that have benefited from a more empowered approach can serve as powerful evidence. Showing the return on investment (ROI) from projects that adhered to true agile principles can help make a compelling business case to higher management and skeptics.

!!!Important note!!!

While exploring the challenges faced by Product Managers within partially adopted SAFe environments, it's essential to clarify that this chapter does not aim to criticize the Scaled Agile Framework (SAFe) itself. This can happen with any framework; I have simply witnessed this with SAFe most often.

When fully embraced, with comprehensive buy-in from all levels of management, SAFe offers a robust structure that can significantly benefit product organizations (I have been SAFe certified for years now and I have worked with many SAFe teams). The framework is designed to align teams, streamline workflows, and foster an environment of continuous delivery and improvement, underpinning the strategic agility companies need to thrive in competitive markets.

However, a critical aspect of SAFe's effectiveness is its call for widespread organizational change. This requirement, demanding a shift in mindset, practices, and culture across the enterprise, is often underestimated or overlooked. The leap from traditional management styles to a genuinely agile, product-centric approach is substantial. Without a commitment to this extensive transformation, attempts to adopt SAFe can result in a mismatch of methodologies and expectations, leaving Product Managers navigating the complexities of an "unSAFE" environment.

The key takeaway here is not to view SAFe or any agile framework as a panacea or a set of prescriptive steps that can be selectively applied. Instead, successful implementation depends on a holistic commitment to the principles of agility and product focus, necessitating organizational readiness to embrace change at all levels. For those considering SAFe, the journey should start with a candid assessment of the organization's willingness and ability to undergo the deep, systemic changes that true agility demands.

Section 2:
Creating a Product Organization

Ch. 16

A Call to Action

As we have journeyed through the intricacies of product management, uncovering the common pitfalls and barriers that restrict product managers and their teams, it's likely that these discussions have resonated with many leaders in companies navigating the digital solution space.

Recognizing these challenges within your organization can be the first step toward transformative change. If you've found that your organization has encountered any of these obstacles, take heart; the next sections of this book are designed with you in mind.

Empowering Your Product Team

In the chapters ahead, we aim to unravel the blueprint for building a formidable, super-powered product team capable of delivering exceptional software solutions. We'll discuss the essence of empowering product managers, providing them with the tools, authority, and environment they need to lead their teams to success.

This isn't just about granting autonomy; it's about nurturing a culture where product managers are seen as the strategic drivers of your digital products.

Leadership's Role in Guiding Success

Your role as a leader is pivotal in ensuring that your product team is not just busy, but productive and aligned with the overarching goals of your business. We'll explore how to establish and leverage Objectives and Key Results (OKRs) and business outcomes to guide your product team's efforts.

This involves working closely with your product managers to ensure that the deliverables are not only achieved but are impactful and contribute meaningfully to the business's success.

Driving Systemic Change

Lastly, we will address how you, as a leader, can instigate and sustain systemic change within your organization. Creating a product-centric culture and empowering your product teams requires more than isolated initiatives; it demands a shift in the organizational hierarchy and mindset.

We'll provide strategies for embedding the product mindset across all levels of your organization, ensuring that empowerment, agility, and innovation become the hallmarks of your company's approach to product development.

Bottom Line

Transforming the way your organization builds and manages digital products is no easy task. It requires commitment, leadership, and a willingness to embrace change. As we move forward, keep in mind that the journey to empowering your product team and adopting a true product mindset is both challenging and rewarding.

The insights and strategies outlined in the following chapters are your roadmap to not only avoiding the pitfalls previously discussed but to achieving a level of product excellence that will set your organization apart in the digital landscape.

Ready to go? Let's get started.

Ch. 17
Getting Started

Embarking on the journey toward a product-focused organization is far more profound and complex than most anticipate. It's not merely about adjusting workflows or introducing new titles like 'Product Manager'—it's about fundamentally rethinking how your organization operates and values its people and products. The symptoms we've discussed throughout this book, from disconnected roadmaps to inefficient delivery, are merely the tip of the iceberg. Beneath the surface lies a dense network of systemic issues that have, over time, fostered a culture of disillusionment among product teams.

For this transformation to take root and flourish, it must be embraced not only by the highest echelons of leadership but must also cascade down through every stratum of the organization. This isn't a superficial change that can be achieved with a few workshops or motivational emails. It demands a sustained commitment to redefining roles, responsibilities, and success metrics across the board.

Our Product Crusaders play a pivotal role in this process, serving as the champions of change at all levels. Their strategic positioning and unwavering dedication to the cause are crucial for ensuring that the principles of a product-centric approach penetrate every corner of the enterprise.

Set Realistic Expectations

However, make no mistake: this is a marathon, not a sprint. Morale will indeed ebb and flow as the organization navigates this seismic shift. There will be moments of backsliding, where the comfort of old habits beckons. It's during these times that the true test of your commitment to change will manifest. By setting clear success criteria and revisiting it regularly, you can keep the organization aligned and focused on the long-term vision. Remember, this transformation is an ongoing endeavor that will demand persistence, resilience, and, most importantly, patience from everyone involved.

Dealing with the Fear:

Overcoming the inertia and fear associated with change requires a deliberate and compassionate approach. Change, by its very nature, is unsettling. It pushes us out of our comfort zones, challenging the status quo and prompting a range of emotional responses. Here, the power of a compelling vision cannot be overstated—it serves as a beacon of hope, illuminating the path to a more promising and efficient future.

Identify Existing Problems

The first step in confronting these fears is to lay bare the issues plaguing your current processes. It's crucial to articulate not only how these problems affect the business's bottom line but also their detrimental impact on customers and the product itself.

Equally important is to voice the personal toll these issues take on your product team. Encouraging team members to share their experiences and struggles provides invaluable insight into the challenges they face and fosters a deeper sense of empathy and unity within the organization.

Provide Meaningful Solutions

With these problems brought to light, the conversation can shift toward solutions. By drawing a clear line from the identified issues to the proposed changes and how they align with the overarching product vision, you create a narrative of transformation. This narrative isn't just about fixing what's broken; it's about striving for something better, for everyone involved—customers, the business, and the team.

A Hopeful Future

This juxtaposition of current pain points against the potential for improvement serves as a powerful motivator. It anchors the need for change in real, relatable terms and connects the dots back to your product vision. This vision isn't merely a lofty ideal; it's a tangible goal that promises a more fulfilling, efficient, and innovative working environment. By framing the transition in this manner, you can help alleviate fears and build a collective enthusiasm for the journey ahead.

Ch. 18

The Time is NOW

The first and most important thing is that leaders impart the value of implementing a product-based framework. Generally, these initiatives are extremely difficult and never get any traction because of the sheer commitment to change.

This is a reality for a company that is working on a well-established consumer facing product as much as it is for a company that only has internal-facing software that supports its own operations.

It is imperative that leadership understands the value and is continually communicating that value. They must be living and dying by the will to make this change. Some of the biggest issues that have been outlined in this book have been a result of adopting 'product', 'agile' or 'scrum' and fundamentally misunderstanding why and how they work in the first place.

Most importantly, the team needs to understand the cost of not making the change. What do we stand to lose by doing nothing and what can be unlocked by making change? How will it benefit the company and by proxy everyone who is involved? Finally, how can we use this as a way to motivate the teams when things aren't so fresh and new?

In order to truly emphasize the importance and value, the following could be done to display the impacts on the business:

- Begin to go through user feedback, find issues that are especially troublesome and bring them to the forefront. How long have they gone ignored? What are the ramifications?

- Take a look at some of your product and developer reviews on a tool like GlassDoor. Are they positive? Maybe highlight high value team members that have left for greener pastures or even worse, your competition

- Introduce the OKRs or business outcomes that will be your guiding light for the product or products that you are building. How will we measure them? Put a plan together on how they will be measured and how we will keep ourselves honest.

- Provide a compelling vision. A Vision is not a set of user features and functionalities. A Vision is a compelling piece of marketing that is designed to inspire our teams to bring value to our users and business. Why should they care about the work?

These are the actions that will get the ball rolling. Your team will now be poised to understand the value and motivated to chase this new goal. Motivation, however, is very fleeting, so it is imperative that leadership be committed and to truly live and breathe the commitment to a more product-centered organization.

Ch. 19

Sustained Leadership Actions

Embarking on a transformation to a product-based framework requires more than just a decision—it demands a relentless commitment from leadership. This commitment is the bedrock upon which all subsequent change efforts are built. It's not just about adopting new labels like 'product' 'agile' or 'scrum'; it's about deeply understanding their essence and integrating their principles into the very fabric of the organization.

Leaders must not only recognize the value of this shift but must be its most vocal champions, continuously articulating the necessity of change. This is true whether the focus is on enhancing a consumer-facing product or optimizing internal software that powers business operations. Leadership's role extends beyond mere endorsement; they must personify the change, demonstrating through their actions and decisions the principles they espouse.

One of the pivotal aspects of fostering a sense of urgency is conveying the stakes—both what stands to be lost by inaction and what can be gained through transformation. Leaders must paint a vivid picture of the potential benefits, not only in terms of business outcomes but also in how it elevates everyone involved in the process. This dual focus on risk and reward serves as a powerful motivator, especially during times when the novelty of change begins to wane.

Making the Case for Change

To underscore the importance and immediate necessity of adopting a product-based framework, leaders can adopt the following strategies:

1. **User Feedback as a Catalyst**: Reviewing user feedback to spotlight long-standing issues that have been overlooked. Question the ramifications of these unresolved problems and use them to illustrate the urgent need for a customer-centric approach.

2. **Reflect on Talent and Reputation**: Examine product and developer reviews on platforms like GlassDoor. Highlight the departure of high-value team members, possibly to competitors, as a wake-up call to address internal shortcomings and improve the organizational culture.

3. **Set and Communicate Clear OKRs**: Introduce Objectives and Key Results (OKRs) or specific business outcomes as the north star for your product initiatives. Outline a transparent method for measuring these outcomes and maintaining accountability throughout the transformation journey.

4. **Craft a Compelling Vision**: Beyond a mere list of features or functionalities, your vision should be an inspiring narrative that motivates the team to strive for excellence. It should articulate the broader impact of their work on users and the company, providing a meaningful context for their efforts.

Leadership in Action: Living the Change

The adage "walk it like you talk it" has never been more pertinent. As a leader, your actions and decisions set the tone for the entire organization. The initial momentum towards change can be exhilarating, yet the true test lies in maintaining this direction without reverting to old, counterproductive habits. It's crucial to remain vigilant against the influence of dominant voices, including your own, that may inadvertently hinder the progress of transformation.

Reflect on the HiPPO (Highest Paid Person's Opinion) phenomenon and ask yourself: Are you becoming an obstacle to your team's success? Leadership isn't about asserting your opinion as the de facto direction; it's about fostering an environment where the best ideas prevail, regardless of their source. Your role is to guide your team with clear business and product goals, providing objective, measurable targets for them to achieve.

Don't Be the Source of a 'Feature Factory'

Every feature request, regardless of its origin, should be treated as a hypothesis that requires validation. This approach ensures that the product team's efforts are aligned with delivering real value to users and achieving strategic business objectives, rather than merely expanding the feature set.

- **Uniform Scrutiny for All Feature Hypotheses**: Each proposed feature, whether inspired internally, by user feedback, or any other source, should be subjected to the same rigorous analysis. Assess its alignment with your Objectives and Key Results (OKRs), its strategic fit within the product roadmap, and its potential to fulfill genuine user needs.

- **Evidence-Based Validation**: Encourage your team to seek out and analyze data, conduct user research, and run experiments to validate the necessity and potential impact of the feature. This evidence-based approach ensures that resources are invested in developments that have a verified premise for success.

- **Strategic Decision Making**: Guide your team to make decisions that are strategically sound, ensuring that new features contribute meaningfully to the product's value proposition and long-term vision. Decisions should be grounded in a deep understanding of user behavior, market trends, and the product's unique strengths.

Leadership's Role in Fostering a Strategic Product Culture

As a leader, your responsibility extends beyond merely endorsing a strategic approach to feature development; you must actively promote a culture that values critical thinking, innovation, and user-centricity.

- **Advocate for a Problem-Solving Mindset**: Reinforce the importance of focusing on solving user problems and meeting their needs effectively. This mindset shifts the narrative from adding features to creating solutions.

- **Promote Transparency and Open Dialogue**: Create an environment where team members feel empowered to question, suggest, and challenge ideas openly. This transparency fosters a collaborative approach to refining hypotheses and aligning on strategic priorities.

- **Champion Continuous Learning and Improvement**: Encourage your teams to embrace a culture of continuous learning, where feedback loops and iterative development are valued. Support initiatives that promote skill enhancement, knowledge sharing, and experimentation.

Ch. 20

Product-Centric Culture

For leaders embarking on the transformative journey of fostering an empowered and autonomous product team, understanding and implementing the basics is pivotal. These foundational elements not only set the stage for success but also ensure that the ensuing cultural shift aligns with the broader objectives of your organization. Here's a primer on the essentials:

Leadership Commitment

- **Top-Down Initiative:** Major cultural shifts must be championed by influential decision-makers at the top. Leadership's commitment to change is crucial for inspiring the rest of the organization.

- **Lead by Example:** It's imperative for leaders to embody the principles they wish to instill in their teams. This means advocating for and practicing the behaviors and values that support product team autonomy and empowerment.

Strategic Empowerment

- **Define Success at the Enterprise Level:** Leaders should clearly articulate what success looks like, aligning it with overarching business goals while entrusting teams with the autonomy to devise and implement solutions.

- **Encourage Best Practices**: Promote practices that foster collaboration, innovation, and efficiency, setting aside any tendencies toward micromanagement or ego-driven decision-making.

Build a Group of Product Crusaders:

This should be a small but very influential group that can be trusted to both lead and believe in your cause. They are sold on the vision and are determined to see it realized. They should be ambitious leaders and performers you can rely on

Identifying Advocates (More in Ch. 24)

- **Diverse Representation**: Select leaders from various departments—product, engineering, marketing, sales, customer success, and finance—to ensure a holistic approach to product development and organizational change.

- **Proven Change Agents**: Look for individuals who have successfully led or championed change initiatives in the past. Their experience and credibility can be invaluable in driving new transformations.

- **Passionate Visionaries**: Include leaders who are genuinely passionate about creating value for customers and empowering teams. Their enthusiasm can inspire and motivate others.

Empowering the Crusade

- **Comprehensive Understanding**: Ensure every member of the group fully grasps the goals and vision behind the move towards an empowered product team model. They should be well-versed in the principles of autonomy, agile methodologies, and customer-centric development.

- **Visible Commitment**: Crusaders must not only endorse the change verbally but also demonstrate their commitment through their actions and decisions. This includes practicing the behaviors they wish to see, such as empowering their teams, advocating for customer insights in decision-making, and supporting continuous learning.

- **Communication and Evangelization**: Equip your Crusaders with the tools and platforms they need to communicate the change effectively. This might include internal presentations, workshops, and regular updates that keep the rest of the organization informed and engaged.

Sustaining Advocacy

- **Feedback Loops**: Establish mechanisms for collecting feedback from across the organization to monitor the impact of the change. The coalition should use this feedback to adjust their strategies and messaging as needed.

- **Recognition and Rewards**: Publicly acknowledge and reward behaviors that align with the new culture of empowerment. This can help reinforce the desired behaviors and encourage widespread adoption.

- **Ongoing Training and Support**: Provide coalition members with continuous opportunities for learning and development. This could involve training sessions, attendance at relevant conferences, or access to resources on leadership and product management best practices.

Seeking External Expertise

- **Product Coaches and Consultants:** Recognizing when external guidance is necessary can be pivotal. A skilled product coach can bridge gaps in understanding and practice, steering the transformation toward success. However, caution is advised in selecting a coach, as the quality and relevance of coaching can vary widely. It's essential to find someone whose expertise and approach genuinely align with your organization's needs and aspirations.

- **Investing in Key Competencies:** For a transformation to succeed, investment in four key competencies is non-negotiable: Product Management, Product Leadership, Product Design (beyond mere aesthetics to real user-centered design), and Technical Leadership that is invested in the 'what' as much as the 'how'. Without a commitment to nurturing these areas, expecting meaningful outcomes from transformation efforts is unrealistic.

Customer-Centric Development

- **Obsession with Customer Problems**: Always prioritize the customer, focusing relentlessly on understanding and solving their problems. Your product's purpose for existing is to address these needs effectively.

- **Collaborative Solutions for Customer Problems:** Through active collaboration with internal stakeholders, we identify the most effective solutions to customer challenges. Our role transcends merely "serving the business"; we're a cohesive unit working in concert with our internal partners to prioritize and address the needs of our customers.

- **Measure What Matters**: Implement metrics that reflect the achievement of business outcomes related to revenue, engagement, customer satisfaction, etc. Ensure these metrics are actionable and regularly reviewed.

- **DevOps: The Silent Assassin**: Often overlooked as a product concern but something that should be considered in empowerment is the role of DevOps. If we do not have a robust DevOps pipeline, then we are tying an arm behind our back. And its absence will make it very difficult to deliver with a tight feedback loop.

Building a Culture of Empowerment and Learning

- **Foster Self-Organizing Teams**: Create an environment where teams are empowered to organize themselves around tasks and challenges, promoting ownership and accountability.

- **Continuous Improvement and Learning**: Encourage a culture where constant learning and adaptation are valued. Invest in opportunities for team growth, such as training, conferences, and networking.

- **Promote a Tight Feedback Loop and Acceptance of Failure**: Establish mechanisms for rapid feedback and learning from failures. Encourage experimentation, ensuring that safety nets are in place for risk mitigation, particularly in sensitive industries.

Ch. 21
Defining Success

The Value of Establishing Business Outcomes

Establishing clear and ambitious business outcomes is more than a strategic exercise; it's a unifying force within an organization. These outcomes serve as a beacon, guiding all teams towards a common goal that transcends individual departmental objectives.

By aligning everyone with these overarching goals, the enterprise ensures that every effort, decision, and initiative contributes towards a shared vision of success.

Unifying Effect

The consensus around business outcomes ensures that everyone, from the top leadership to individual contributors, understands what the organization values most. This shared understanding fosters a culture where the pursuit of these goals becomes a collective endeavor, prioritizing the organization's needs over any single team's agenda.

Navigating Stakeholder Contentiousness

In moments of disagreement or conflict—whether between different stakeholder groups or between stakeholders and the product team—established business outcomes serve as a critical reference point. They act as a neutral ground for discussions, helping to refocus debates on what will best serve the overarching objectives of the organization. **When decisions need to be made, these outcomes provide a clear criterion: does this action or feature directly contribute to achieving our defined goals?**

A Tool for Prioritization

Moreover, business outcomes become invaluable in prioritization. In the face of limited resources and time, they help clarify which initiatives, features, or projects will deliver the most significant impact towards the organization's strategic goals. This prioritization ensures efficient allocation of resources, focusing efforts on what truly matters to the business's success.

Enhancing Stakeholder Collaboration

By establishing a common set of outcomes, the organization encourages collaboration and breaks down silos. Teams are more likely to seek cross-functional partnerships and share insights when they recognize how their collective efforts contribute to a larger purpose.

This collaborative environment not only accelerates progress towards shared goals but also fosters innovation and creativity by bringing diverse perspectives together in pursuit of common objectives.

Empowering Through Objective Measures

Challenge decisions that veer away from the established goals. It's essential that every decision, particularly those affecting the product's direction, is scrutinized and supported by data. Ideas, even those originating from the highest levels of leadership, must be treated as hypotheses to be validated or refuted based on evidence.

Encourage your team to seek and present data to back their proposals, fostering a culture where data-driven decision-making is the norm. This not only elevates the quality of discussions and decisions but also empowers team members to contribute meaningfully, knowing that their ideas will be considered on their merits.

Ch. 22

Measuring Success

Establishing Goals and OKRs

Objective and Key Results (OKRs) represent a cornerstone in the architecture of goal setting and performance measurement within organizations. OKRs are designed to help teams align their efforts towards achieving significant impacts on the business. It's about setting ambitious goals (Objectives) and tracking their outcomes with tangible metrics (Key Results).

The Purpose of OKRs

OKRs serve a dual purpose: guiding teams towards high-level organizational goals while allowing flexibility in the methods used to achieve them. This framework encourages innovation, accountability, and transparency across all levels of an organization, ensuring everyone is moving in the same direction with clarity and purpose.

Examples of OKRs

Here are a few examples that illustrate how OKRs might be structured within different contexts:

1. **Objective: Increase Market Share in the XYZ segment.**

- **Key Result 1:** Launch two new product features tailored to the XYZ segment's needs by Q2.
- **Key Result 2:** Achieve a 15% increase in new sign-ups from the XYZ segment by Q3.
- **Key Result 3:** Improve customer satisfaction scores within the XYZ segment to 90% by Q4.

2. **Objective: Boost Overall Revenue.**
   - **Key Result 1:** Increase average subscription size by 20% by the end of the year.
   - **Key Result 2:** Reduce churn rate to less than 5% per quarter.
   - **Key Result 3:** Open two new sales channels by Q3.

3. **Objective: Enhance Customer Satisfaction.**
   - **Key Result 1:** Reduce average customer service response time to under 2 hours.
   - **Key Result 2:** Implement a customer feedback loop and achieve a product improvement rating of 80% based on feedback.
   - **Key Result 3:** Launch a customer education program resulting in a 25% increase in customer engagement metrics.

Comparing and Contrasting KPIs and OKRs

While both KPIs (Key Performance Indicators) and OKRs are vital tools for measuring performance and success, they serve different purposes and are used in complementary ways:

- **KPIs** are metrics that provide insights into the ongoing performance of various aspects of the business. They are often used to monitor the health of the business, ensuring it operates within expected parameters.
- **OKRs**, on the other hand, are goal-setting frameworks that help define and track objectives and their outcomes. OKRs are typically

more dynamic, focusing on specific goals for a set period, encouraging growth and improvement.

While KPIs might tell you where the problem areas are, OKRs are about setting and achieving forward-looking goals that can move the needle for the business.

Examples of KPIs

1. **Customer Acquisition Cost (CAC):** The total cost of acquiring a new customer, crucial for understanding the efficiency of marketing efforts.

2. **Lifetime Value (LTV):** The total revenue expected from a customer over their lifetime, indicating the long-term value of customer relationships.

3. **Net Promoter Score (NPS):** A measure of customer loyalty and satisfaction, providing insights into the customer's willingness to recommend the product or service.

Ch. 23

The Essence of the Product Vision

At the heart of every transformative product journey lies a compelling vision, a beacon that illuminates the path for the entire organization. This vision encapsulates not just the aspirations for the product but embodies the very reason behind every effort, decision, and innovation. It is the fundamental narrative that binds the team's ambitions and guides their strategic direction.

Anatomy of a Vision: Crafting a Future to Believe In

A product vision should be audacious, perhaps bordering on the visionary, painting a picture of the future where users' needs are not just met but exceeded. This isn't about setting short-term targets; it's about projecting a future that stretches years ahead, where the product has evolved to solve problems so effectively that users can't imagine their lives without it.

More Than the Sum of Its Parts

The vision serves as the primary source of motivation for your team, instilling a belief that they are contributing to something greater than the immediate tasks at hand. It's about building a legacy, not just ticking off checkboxes. In essence, the team isn't merely stacking bricks; they're crafting a cathedral, each brick laid with purpose and foresight towards a grand design.

Letter from the Future: A Visioning Exercise

A practical and powerful exercise to kickstart the visioning process is the 'Letter from the Future.' This exercise involves writing a letter to yourself or your team from a future standpoint, describing the product in its ideal state.

Imagine the nuances of running your business with the product as it should be, detailing who it serves, its role in supporting business objectives, and how success is measured. Envision the rave reviews from customers and the vibrant dynamics of your team working at their best.

This narrative exercise does more than just aid in synthesizing a vision; it helps in grounding your aspirations in tangible outcomes, making the vision relatable and inspiring for the entire team.

The Vision as a Guiding Light

A well-articulated product vision transcends the realm of mere functionality or feature sets; it encapsulates the essence of the impact your product aspires to have on the world. It's a clarion call that rallies your team, aligns stakeholders, and serves as a constant reminder of the why behind your what.

In crafting this vision, remember that its power lies not in its precision but in its ability to inspire, motivate, and guide. It's about setting a direction that feels almost out of reach but is worth every effort to strive towards. This vision becomes the narrative that every team member, leader, and stakeholder can embrace and work towards, turning ambitious dreams into tangible realities.

Ch. 24

Product Crusaders

Embarking on the bold path of reshaping our approach to empower product teams, we must widen our lens beyond the immediate circle crafting our digital products. This transformation journey transcends the confines of just the product managers, developers, and designers.

It encompasses the entire ecosystem within which the product team operates, drawing in sales, marketing, product marketing, finance, and, crucially, executive leadership.

The linchpin to steering this ship of change isn't solely in the hands of those at the product helm. It equally depends on the commitment and understanding from every corner of the business that touches, influences, or benefits from the product's success. If these vital segments of our organization aren't fully aligned—ensuring that the product requirements, priorities, and outcomes are cohesively managed—the noble quest of our product teams could falter before it truly begins.

This is where our 'Product Crusaders' come into the narrative. This isn't just a fancy title; it's a call to arms for a select group, champions from every business vertical who are ready to stand behind this change with vigor and conviction. They're the bridge builders, the advocates who carry the torch of transformation into every discussion, meeting, and strategy session. Their role transcends mere support; they're active participants ensuring that the vision of an empowered product team is not a solitary struggle but a shared organizational ambition.

The Formation of Product Crusaders

In the echelons just beneath the pinnacle of leadership, there exists a cadre of influential decision-makers and stakeholders whose advocacy is crucial for nurturing a product-centric organization. This collective, dubbed the 'Product Crusaders,' plays a pivotal role in championing the ethos of product enablement, acting as the vanguard that encourages teams to embrace and trust the leadership and processes of the product team.

Assembling Your Coalition

From sales and finance to product marketing, design, and even the executive team, each member must be a fervent believer in the value of the product team's work, tirelessly advocating for its adoption across the company. They wield their influence not just through their hierarchical standing but also through their ability to inspire and guide organizational change.

Empowering the Crusaders

Training is just the starting point for empowering your Product Crusaders. They may need insights from external consultants or a dedicated coach to fully grasp the expected functioning of a product organization. Their understanding should cover the expected behaviors, delivery mechanisms, and operational ethos of the product team, aligned with the overarching vision.

Commitment goes beyond education; these Crusaders must embody the product mindset, even when it challenges existing norms. This might mean prioritizing long-term value over short-term gains for sales, or for leaders, tempering their ego to amplify the collective voice of the product team.

Sustaining the Momentum

Change, while necessary, is inherently challenging. Without consistent effort to reinforce this new direction, it's all too easy for individuals to revert to familiar patterns, especially under pressure or uncertainty. Establishing regular touchpoints—whether weekly or bi-weekly—where Crusaders can address emerging challenges ensures that minor obstacles don't snowball into major roadblocks.

Recognition plays a crucial role in sustaining advocacy. Celebrate the successes of teams who exemplify the change, highlighting the positive impact on customers and, eventually, on the bottom line. Such acknowledgment not only bolsters morale but also solidifies the value of the shift towards a product-focused culture.

Continuous Learning and Improvement

The landscape of product management is ever-evolving, making an environment of continuous learning and adaptation non-negotiable. Encourage your Crusaders to pursue further education, offer incentives for skill advancement, and bring in expert voices through seminars and guest speakers. Keeping abreast of the latest in product development and management ensures your Crusaders, and through them, your entire organization, remains at the cutting edge of innovation and efficiency.

In crafting this legion of Product Crusaders, you're not just building a team; you're cultivating a movement within your organization. One that champions the cause of product management with zeal and unwavering conviction, guiding your teams toward a future where product excellence is not just envisioned but realized.

Ch. 25

Embracing Customer Centricity

One of the cornerstone principles within any product organization worth its salt is a steadfast commitment to customer-centric development. But what does it truly mean to be customer-centric in the context of developing products?

The Essence of Customer-Centric Development

At its heart, customer-centric development is an approach where every decision, from the initial spark of an idea to the delivery of the final product, is made with the customer's welfare front and center.

It's about more than just meeting needs; it's about actively improving customers' lives through the solutions we build. This commitment to serving and solving problems for the customer drives innovation, adaptability, and ultimately, value.

Practicing Customer Empathy

How do we operationalize this ideology? Through an unwavering dedication to understanding and alleviating customer problems. Customer empathy should be the pulse of the development process, reminding us at every step that the customer is not just a passive recipient but the very reason for our product's existence.

Collaborative Decision-Making

This customer-first mindset necessitates a collaborative approach between product teams and stakeholders (see Ch. 31). It challenges the traditional dynamic where stakeholders might dictate features based on internal goals rather than customer needs.

Here, the product team emerges as the customer's champion, advocating for solutions that truly serve, even if it means shifting long-standing power dynamics within the organization.

For some organizations, this shift towards empowering product teams to make customer-centric decisions may feel like uncharted territory. Sales teams or executive leadership may be accustomed to directing the product agenda.

It's dependent on both product professionals and leadership to underscore the importance of aligning with business outcomes that serve the broader vision and the customer, moving beyond the 'squeaky wheel' approach to prioritization.

The Role of Business Stakeholders in Solutioning

Business stakeholders, with their unique insights into market dynamics, customer behavior, and business objectives, are invaluable to the product development process. Their role transcends the mere provision of requirements or demands for specific features.

Instead, stakeholders are best positioned to articulate the challenges and problems faced by customers, drawing on their direct interactions and strategic vantage points.

By bringing these problems to the product team, stakeholders act as the voice of the customer, ensuring that the product strategy remains responsive to real needs and opportunities.

Embracing a Problem-Based Approach

The approach to decision-making within this collaborative framework should be unequivocally problem-centric. This means prioritizing the identification and understanding of customer problems over prescribing specific solutions. The rationale behind this is twofold:

1. **Empowerment through Trust**: By entrusting the product team with the responsibility to devise solutions, stakeholders demonstrate confidence in the team's expertise, creativity, and understanding of the product vision. This trust empowers product teams to explore innovative solutions, experiment, and iterate, ultimately leading to more effective and user-centered outcomes.

2. **Leveraging Diverse Expertise**: The product team, equipped with a multi-faceted view encompassing UX design, technical capabilities, and market trends, is in an ideal position to translate complex customer problems into viable product features. Their solutioning process is enriched by diverse perspectives, ensuring that the resulting product resonates with users and aligns with business goals.

The Collaborative Dynamic

The dynamic between business stakeholders and the product team should be characterized by open dialogue, shared understanding, and a commitment to collaboration.

Stakeholders provide the context and articulate the *problems*, setting the stage for the product team to apply its expertise in crafting solutions.

This collaborative model fosters a culture of innovation, where problem-solving drives product development, and customer needs are met with ingenuity and precision.

Ch. 26
What's Important NOW

Leadership's Influence on Prioritization: Guiding Success Through Strategic Outcomes

In the realm of product development, the compass that guides a team towards impactful work isn't just about understanding success; it's about defining what success looks like through the lens of strategic outcomes. Leadership plays a pivotal role in this process, not by dictating every move but by setting clear priorities based on a thorough understanding of what outcomes matter the most. This prioritization is more than a hierarchical list; it's a strategic decision-making process grounded in validation and measurable success.

The Crucial Role of Measurement

At the core of meaningful product development lies a robust framework of analytics and success metrics. It's this data-driven backbone that transforms every feature from a hypothesis to a measurable impact. Without this, we venture into the realm of subjectivity, where decisions are swayed by anecdotes rather than hard evidence.

KPIs and OKRs: The Twin Beacons of Success

The symbiosis between Key Performance Indicators (KPIs) at the feature level and broader Objectives and Key Results (OKRs) is where the magic happens. OKRs chart the course for the organization's strategic goals, laying down the markers for success. The alignment of KPIs with these OKRs ensures that every feature developed isn't just a tick on the product roadmap but a step towards achieving overarching business goals.

This alignment is pivotal, transforming the product development narrative from a feature-centric approach to an outcome-centric one. It's not just about what features are delivered but how these features move the needle on the organization's key results, driving growth and enhancing customer satisfaction.

Strategic Prioritization: A Deliberate Exercise

With a clear alignment between KPIs and OKRs, prioritization becomes a strategic exercise. Features that resonate with the organization's goals and boast impactful KPIs are given precedence. This methodology effectively counters the risk of falling into the trap of prioritizing based on vocal advocacy rather than strategic value.

In this model, stakeholders play a crucial role by offering insights and championing the needs of their respective domains. However, the final arbiter of value and priority remains the product team, equipped with data and aligned with the organization's strategic objectives. This ensures that product development is laser-focused on delivering not just solutions but solutions that propel the business forward, achieving the most critical outcomes.

Ch. 27

What is a Product Team?

In navigating the complexities of modern product development, it's essential to clarify the terminology and framework that will guide our discussion throughout this book. Central to our approach is the concept of the Product Team, a term that encompasses more than just a group of individuals working on a product. It signifies a holistic approach to defining the strategic direction and tactical execution of product solutions. Simultaneously, we embrace the Agile framework as the methodology governing the 'how'—the actual delivery and implementation of these solutions. This bifurcation between the 'what' and 'why,' and the 'how,' forms the backbone of our advocated model for product development.

The Product Team: Defining the What and Why

The Product Team is the cornerstone of product development, responsible for identifying user needs, conceptualizing solutions, and setting the strategic vision for the product. This team is not siloed by function but is cross-disciplinary, bringing together expertise from product management, design, engineering, and more, to ensure a multifaceted approach to problem-solving. Their collective responsibility is to determine 'what' needs to be built and 'why' it is valuable—both to the user and the business.

The 'what' encompasses the features, functionalities, and user experiences that will be developed. It's defined not by whims but by a rigorous understanding of user needs, market dynamics, and business objectives. The 'why' delves into the rationale behind each decision, ensuring that every aspect of the product is purposefully aligned with solving real problems and achieving measurable outcomes.

Agile as the Framework for How

Once the 'what' and 'why' are established by the Product Team, the focus shifts to 'how' these strategic visions and tactical plans will be brought to fruition. This is where the Agile framework comes into play, providing the methodologies and practices for efficient, iterative, and flexible product development. Agile is not just a set of processes but a mindset that emphasizes collaboration, customer feedback, and the ability to adapt to changing requirements.

Adopting Agile allows the Product Team to operationalize their strategy through a series of iterative cycles or sprints. This approach ensures that product development is responsive to user feedback and market changes, allowing for continuous refinement and improvement. Agile practices empower teams to break down complex projects into manageable tasks, prioritize them based on value and urgency, and deliver incremental progress towards the product vision.

Product Teams within an Agile Framework

This book strongly advocates for assembling Product Teams that are empowered to determine the 'what' and 'why' of product development, while fully endorsing the Agile framework to guide the 'how.' This dual focus aims to combine strategic vision with tactical agility, ensuring that product solutions are not only conceived with intent but are also implemented with flexibility and responsiveness.

By aligning the strategic focus of Product Teams with the operational efficiency of Agile methodologies, organizations can create a dynamic ecosystem for product development. This model promotes a balanced approach where strategic objectives guide development efforts, and Agile practices provide the framework for executing those strategies effectively.

In essence, this integrated approach seeks to optimize the entire product development lifecycle, ensuring that teams are equipped to deliver solutions that meet user needs, drive business value, and adapt to the ever-evolving landscape of technology and market demands.

Let's dive a little bit deeper into the super powered customer satisfaction that can be unlocked by a proper Product Team.

Product Teams: Architects of Value

Mission-Driven Composition: Product Teams are formulated with a singular, clear mission: to address and solve real-world problems for their users while delivering substantial business value. This mission propels every aspect of their operation, ensuring that each member, regardless of their function, is aligned towards a unified goal.

Autonomy and Empowerment: The autonomy granted to Product Teams is not merely procedural but foundational to their ability to innovate and adapt. It allows them to make informed decisions that are deeply rooted in an understanding of customer needs, market trends, and the overarching vision for the product.

Shared Responsibility: Within a Product Team, responsibility for the product's success is collective. This shared accountability ensures that strategies and solutions are the product of collaborative thinking and expertise, leveraging diverse perspectives to drive value.

The Core of Product Teams: Problem Solving

Problem-Centric Focus: The defining characteristic of a Product Team is its relentless pursuit of problem-solving. This focus shifts the narrative from merely adding features to creating solutions that address specific user pain points and aspirations, thereby ensuring relevance and value.

Strategic Alignment with OKRs: The integration of Objectives and Key Results (OKRs) within the Product Team's workflow is pivotal. OKRs help in setting and tracking focused goals, thereby aligning the team's efforts with the strategic objectives of the business and ensuring that every initiative contributes meaningfully to overarching goals.

Driving Value Through Understanding

Decoding the 'Why': The significance of understanding the 'why' behind every feature cannot be overstated. This deep dive into the rationale behind features ensures that the team's efforts are not just about building solutions but about solving the right problems in ways that genuinely benefit users and align with business strategies.

Creating Measurable Impact: At the heart of a Product Team's mission is the creation of tangible value. This value transcends theoretical benefits, manifesting in real revenue and measurable impact on the company's bottom line, through solutions that directly address and resolve key user problems.

Culture of Innovation

Continuous Innovation and Learning: The culture within a Product Team fosters an environment of continuous innovation, experimentation, and learning. This ethos ensures that the team remains agile, responsive to user feedback, and aligned with the dynamic needs of the market.

Ch. 28

Why do you Need One?

Product Teams: Architects of Value

Mission-Driven Composition: Product Teams are formulated with a singular, clear mission: to address and solve real-world problems for their users while delivering substantial business value. This mission propels every aspect of their operation, ensuring that each member, regardless of their function, is aligned towards a unified goal.

Autonomy and Empowerment: The autonomy granted to Product Teams is not merely procedural but foundational to their ability to innovate and adapt. It allows them to make informed decisions that are deeply rooted in an understanding of customer needs, market trends, and the overarching vision for the product.

Shared Responsibility: Within a Product Team, responsibility for the product's success is collective. This shared accountability ensures that strategies and solutions are the product of collaborative thinking and expertise, leveraging diverse perspectives to drive value.

The Core of Product Teams: Problem Solving

Problem-Centric Focus: The defining characteristic of a Product Team is its relentless pursuit of problem-solving. This focus shifts the narrative from merely adding features to creating solutions that address specific user pain points and aspirations, thereby ensuring relevance and value.

Strategic Alignment with OKRs: The integration of Objectives and Key Results (OKRs) within the Product Team's workflow is pivotal. OKRs help in setting and tracking focused goals, thereby aligning the team's efforts with the strategic objectives of the business and ensuring that every initiative contributes meaningfully to overarching goals.

Driving Value Through Understanding

Decoding the 'Why': The significance of understanding the 'why' behind every feature cannot be overstated. This deep dive into the rationale behind features ensures that the team's efforts are not just about building solutions but about solving the right problems in ways that genuinely benefit users and align with business strategies.

Creating Measurable Impact: At the heart of a Product Team's mission is the creation of tangible value. This value transcends theoretical benefits, manifesting in real revenue and measurable impact on the company's bottom line, through solutions that directly address and resolve key user problems.

Culture of Innovation

Continuous Innovation and Learning: The culture within a Product Team fosters an environment of continuous innovation, experimentation, and learning. This ethos ensures that the team remains agile, responsive to user feedback, and aligned with the dynamic needs of the market.

Ch. 29

Product Team Players

Understanding the composition of your Product Team is essential for fostering a collaborative environment where each role contributes to the discovery and delivery of your product. While everyone on the team plays a crucial part, it's important to recognize the distinct contributions of each role:

Product Manager: The Captain of the Ship

Often (but not always) referred to as the "CEO" of the product, the Product Manager is the linchpin of the Product Team. They drive the vision, strategy, and roadmap, ensuring that every aspect of the product aligns with user needs and business goals. The Product Manager navigates between various stakeholders, synthesizing feedback, market research, and business requirements into a coherent product direction. They are responsible for prioritizing features, setting objectives, and defining the key results that will measure the product's success.

UX/Product Design: The User Advocate

The UX Design team goes beyond crafting wireframes and user interfaces; they are the champions of the user's experience. By directly interacting with users, conducting usability tests, and gathering feedback, UX designers ensure that the product is intuitive, accessible, and delightful to use. They play a critical role in translating user needs into design solutions that enhance user satisfaction and drive engagement.

Development Team: The Builders

The Development Team brings the product vision to life. Comprising developers, QA engineers (if present), and other technical professionals like analysts and architects, this group is responsible for the technical execution of the product. They work closely with the Product Manager and UX Designers to understand the requirements and constraints, implementing the features and functionalities that make up the product. Their expertise in software development, testing, and deployment is essential for delivering a high-quality product that meets both user expectations and technical standards.

Leaders and Stakeholders: The Business Anchors

Leaders and stakeholders, including executives and department heads, serve as key voices in defining the business goals and outcomes that the product aims to achieve. They may also act as proxies for the voice of the customer, particularly in B2B contexts where direct user feedback is channeled through business relationships. While they contribute to setting the strategic direction, they entrust the Product Team with the autonomy to make informed decisions on how best to achieve these goals.

Here are some other potential players that some (but not all) teams may leverage to build World-Class products:

- **Customer Success and Support Teams**: Offer direct user feedback and support insights.
- **Marketing and Sales**: Provide market insights, customer needs, and competitive intelligence.
- **Data Analysts or Data Scientists**: Analyze user data, market trends, and performance metrics.

- **Operations and Infrastructure**: Ensure product feasibility and alignment with operational capabilities.
- **Compliance and Legal**: Guide on compliance, privacy, and legal standards.
- **External Consultants or Experts**: Offer specialized knowledge in specific industries or technologies.
- **Finance**: Align product development with financial goals and budget constraints.

Collaboration as the Key

The strength of a Product Team lies not just in the skills and expertise of its members, but in how effectively they collaborate towards a common vision. Each role contributes a unique perspective, ensuring that the product is well-rounded, strategically aligned, and technically sound. By fostering open communication and mutual respect among Product Managers, UX Designers, Developers, and Stakeholders, the team can navigate challenges, adapt to changes, and deliver a product that truly meets the needs of its users and the objectives of the business.

Ch. 30

Building the Team

Recruiting for a product-focused organization goes beyond assessing skills on a resume; it involves identifying individuals whose attitudes and mindsets align with the foundational principles of product management. This chapter doesn't aim to be an exhaustive manual on assembling a product team from scratch but rather offers insights into selecting candidates who will not just fill a role but thrive within a product-centric culture.

When scouting for talent, the focus should be on identifying those with a genuine passion for solving user problems, a keen ability to embrace change, and a collaborative spirit that elevates the team. Candidates should exhibit a curiosity that drives them to understand the 'why' behind their work, coupled with the resilience to navigate the uncertainties inherent in product development.

Attributes like empathy for the customer, a commitment to continuous learning, and the ability to balance strategic vision with tactical execution are invaluable. These qualities ensure that the team members you bring on board are not just capable of doing the job but are motivated by the right reasons – delivering exceptional value to users and contributing to the business's success.

In this pursuit, interviews and interactions with potential hires should understand the scenarios that reveal their approach to problem-solving, their reactions to feedback and setbacks, and their thoughts on collaboration and leadership. It's through these discussions that you'll glean insights into their fit within a product-driven organization, ensuring that the team you build is not just skilled but aligned in vision and values.

Staffing and Recruiting for Product Mastery

In charting the course for effective staffing and recruiting within the product management ecosystem, understanding and defining the roles becomes the cornerstone of assembling a team capable of turning visions into reality. Here's how to navigate the hiring landscape to ensure your team is poised for success.

1. Tailor the Interview Process with Precision and Purpose

- **Define Responsibilities with Clarity**: Before stepping into the recruitment phase, it's crucial for hiring managers to meticulously outline the role's responsibilities. These should be informed by both the immediate needs of the product and the strategic direction of the organization. A well-defined role is the first step in attracting the right talent.

- **Relevance in Evaluation**: Craft an interview process that reflects the actual challenges and opportunities of the position. Ensure exercises and questions are directly tied to the responsibilities and expectations outlined, valuing both the candidate's time and the authenticity of the evaluation process.

2. Avoid the 'Unicorn' Hiring Pitfall

- **Seek Specific Skills and Experience**: Target your search to candidates whose skills and experience align with the clearly defined needs of the role. Resist the allure of the 'unicorn' candidate who promises to fulfill every conceivable need.

- **Set Realistic Role Expectations**: Recognize the distinction and depth of the product management role. If the job description starts spanning multiple disciplines, consider whether additional roles need to be filled rather than seeking a single individual to cover a broad spectrum of duties.

Broadening the Interview Scope: Vision Alignment and Passion

- **Introduce the Product Vision**: Part of the interview should involve sharing the product's vision with the candidate. This serves not just as an informational exchange but as a litmus test for the candidate's alignment and enthusiasm for the vision. Does it inspire them? Do they show genuine interest in contributing to this vision?

- **Assess Passion for Product**: Beyond skills and experience, gauge the candidate's passion for products and their belief in the power of a product organization. A candidate's enthusiasm for the product and its potential impact can be a significant driver of success, fostering a culture of excitement and commitment among new hires.

Ch. 31

The Collaboration Imperative

Bridging the Divide:

In the labyrinth of most enterprise environments, a conspicuous divide often exists between the technical and business realms. Here, technical teams are frequently seen as mere executors of business ideas, tasked with translating stakeholder visions into tangible solutions.

This dynamic relegates technical teams to a subservient role, where they're expected to deliver based on guidelines that, while well-intentioned, can often seem arbitrary and disconnected from the practical realities of product development.

The Pitfalls of the Over-powered Stakeholder

A Carousel of Changing Objectives: The whims of leadership, customer feedback, or competitive pressures can swiftly alter project trajectories, leaving teams scrambling to adjust.

This reactionary approach can derail carefully laid plans and introduce inefficiencies that are detrimental to product progress.

Ambiguity in Ownership and Prioritization: This model fosters an environment of uncertainty, particularly regarding who truly "owns" the product vision and prioritization.

Product leaders find themselves in a rut, uncertain whether the directive of the day will come from an executive, a customer request, or a sudden shift in market dynamics.

The result is a dilution of the product team's ability to steer the product strategy effectively, often leading to a fragmented and incoherent product experience.

Advocating for a Collaborative Model

To surmount these challenges, a shift towards a more collaborative model is imperative—a model where the generation of ideas and the articulation of problems are shared responsibilities between stakeholders and technical teams. In this paradigm, priorities and objectives are not dictated but discussed, with the product team playing a pivotal role in navigating these conversations.

Empowering Product Teams: At the core of this collaborative ethos is the empowerment of product teams to take ownership of the product backlog and prioritization process.

This doesn't mean operating in isolation but engaging in a dialogue where ideas, challenges, and solutions are openly shared and debated.

The Essence of True Collaboration

The path to a more effective and harmonious working relationship between business stakeholders and product teams lies in fostering a dynamic characterized by mutual respect, open dialogue, and a shared commitment to collaboration. This model acknowledges the unique contributions of each party:

- **Stakeholders** articulate the broader context and highlight problems or opportunities based on their understanding of market needs, business objectives, and customer feedback.
    - Their role is to set the stage by providing the product team with a clear picture of the challenges and goals that the product aims to address.

- **Product Teams** bring their expertise to the fore, applying their deep knowledge of technology, user experience, and market trends to devise innovative solutions.
  - Armed with the insights provided by stakeholders, they set on a creative and analytical journey to turn problems into opportunities to drive customer value.

This collaborative model transcends the limitations of antiquated hierarchical dynamics, fostering an environment where innovation takes precedence.

It's a partnership where problem-solving becomes the driving force behind product development, ensuring that solutions are not only technically feasible but also sharply focused on meeting and exceeding customer expectations.

By embracing this collaborative dynamic, organizations can cultivate a culture of innovation and agility. It's a shift from a world where product teams are mere executors of predefined ideas to one where they are active participants in shaping the product's direction.

This approach ensures that the solutions developed are not only aligned with the business's strategic objectives but are also crafted with the ingenuity and precision that come from a deep, collaborative understanding of customer needs.

Ch. 32

Navigating the Seas of Disagreement

In the complex ecosystem of product development, navigating disagreements is akin to steering a ship through occasionally stormy waters. Conflicts and differing opinions are inevitable, but it's how we manage these disagreements that can make or break the success of a project. Here, we go into common issues and strategies for mitigating them, ensuring that even when the seas get rough, our ship continues towards its destination: delivering value to customers while aligning with overarching business goals.

When Priorities Shift

The question of "Are we working on the most important thing?" frequently arises, especially in highly competitive environments. A sudden idea or market shift can challenge the established priority list and roadmap. Here's how to keep the ship on course:

- **Validation Over Dismissal**: No idea is too outlandish to consider, but every idea requires validation. It's crucial to ensure that new suggestions will have the desired impact before allowing them to alter our course.

- **Alignment with Company Goals**: Every idea must be weighed against our collective understanding of the company's objectives. If an idea doesn't align, regardless of its potential value, it may need to be shelved for a time when it fits better within the strategic framework.

Condemning the Process: The Gatekeeper Dilemma

The product team, in its role as validator of ideas, may sometimes be perceived as a gatekeeper, particularly when stakeholders are anxious to move forward based on the perceived "cost of not doing it." Here's how to address this challenge:

- **Trust in the Process:** It's crucial to stand firm on the principle that no initiative moves forward without evidence that it will yield the desired outcomes. This stance is not about obstruction but about ensuring every step we take is purposeful and impactful.

- **Highlighting the Cost of Unvalidated Action:** In moments of pushback, it's important to articulate the risks of proceeding without validation. Point out that diverting resources to unproven initiatives not only delays other strategic priorities but also poses the risk of investing in solutions that may not deliver the expected benefits. Sharing past instances where premature action led to costly missteps can underscore the importance of this approach.

- **Leverage Product Crusaders:** In times of dissent, expect that Product Crusaders will advocate for the product team's principles, transforming "gatekeeper" criticisms into opportunities for reinforcing the importance of disciplined, validation-first development processes.

The art of managing disagreements within the realm of product development is a testament to the delicate balance between innovation and discipline. By validating ideas, ensuring alignment with strategic goals, and navigating conflicts of interest with a focus on the larger vision, we can foster an environment where collaboration thrives.

Standing firm on the process of validation, especially in the face of pressure to act hastily, reinforces our commitment to making informed, strategic decisions that drive meaningful outcomes for our business and our customers.

Resolving Stakeholder Conflicts

Conflicts of interest between different stakeholder groups, such as the natural tension between compliance or security teams and revenue-focused departments like sales or marketing, are commonplace. The product team often finds itself in the role of mediator, balancing these interests to maintain forward momentum.

- **Risk and Compliance Thresholds**: Establishing clear thresholds for risk and compliance within the OKRs and business outcomes is essential. These thresholds should inform leadership's decision-making, helping to balance innovation with necessary safeguards.
- **Common Goals**: Reminding all parties that we share the same overarching goals is crucial during contentious discussions. When disagreements arise, refocusing on the shared objectives and the business outcomes that benefit everyone can help smooth over conflicts.
- **We Hear You**: When navigating the contentious waters, it is important to remind stakeholders that although some features and solutions serve to support the opposing group, there are others that align with their direct goals.
- **Empathy and Understanding**: Fostering an environment of empathy, where each group's concerns and contributions are acknowledged and valued, can transform potential conflicts into opportunities for innovative, holistic solutions.

Personal Story Time:

Navigating the stormy waters of stakeholder conflicts often reveals deeper undercurrents of misaligned objectives within an organization. A vivid illustration of this can be seen in the tale of two opposing forces within a business:

The fraud management team, armed with an arsenal of security measures, and the sales team, guardians of the customer pipeline and revenue streams. This clash of titans unfolded within the confines of a project focused on integrating a new suite of fraud prevention and know-your-customer (KYC) tools for a POS payment system—a scenario as ubiquitous in the business world as morning coffee runs.

The crux of the conflict revolved around the new customer onboarding processes necessitated by fraud prevention efforts. These procedures, though essential for securing transactions, presented a spectrum of customer friction, with the intensity level directly tied to our risk appetite. The fraud management team, with their sights set on fortifying our defenses, pushed for a stringent approach.

However, each additional layer of security, each hoop through which customers were asked to jump, threatened to throttle the flow of potential revenue, igniting fierce resistance from the sales team, whose primary focus lay in smoothing the path to purchase for potential customers.

This classic confrontation underscored a prevalent issue: the creation of departmental goals in isolation, devoid of a comprehensive vision for the enterprise. Triggered by an industry-wide data breach, our engagement was primarily a knee-jerk reaction from the cybersecurity leadership, amplifying the disconnect between the impetus for enhanced security and the continuous drive for sales growth.

In the short term, we navigated the impasse by defining a balanced threshold of risk acceptable to both teams. This compromise meant acknowledging that while we couldn't vet every lead with an impossibly high standard of perfection, we also couldn't open the floodgates to potential fraud. The consensus on a middle ground provided a temporary peace, allowing business to proceed without paralyzing safeguards or reckless exposure.

The real breakthrough, however, came in the long-term strategy adjustments. This scenario spotlighted the necessity for overarching product goals and unified business outcomes. It prompted a pivotal shift in our planning process. Before the next cycle, we tasked management with setting clear, quantifiable objectives: concrete sales revenue targets, defined thresholds for fraud tolerance, and benchmarks for fraud detection success.

Equipped with these comprehensive guidelines, we were empowered to craft a roadmap that was not only more aligned with the enterprise's strategic aims but also more attuned to our users' needs. By balancing ease of onboarding and robust security, we charted a course towards a service experience that was both accessible and safe. This strategic realignment demonstrated the power of holistic planning in harmonizing divergent priorities, guiding us towards solutions that served both our business objectives and our commitment to customer trust and satisfaction.

As we embark on the next section of our journey, "Autonomy Found: Empowering Product Professionals," we lay out the essential steps required to not only foster an environment conducive to autonomy but also to ensure our product professionals are equipped with the necessary skills and tools to thrive within it.

This section is dedicated to transforming competent individuals into solution-oriented problem solvers, passionately committed to innovation and continuous improvement.

Cultivating Capabilities and Skills

At the heart of a truly autonomous product professional lies a diverse set of capabilities and skills that go beyond traditional product management knowledge. These include strategic thinking, empathetic user understanding, data-driven decision-making, and adeptness at navigating complex stakeholder landscapes. Our focus will be on practical strategies to nurture these competencies, including hands-on exercises, real-world problem-solving scenarios, and mentorship opportunities that challenge and expand their thinking.

Equipping with the Right Tools

Beyond skill development, providing a robust toolkit is crucial for optimizing success. This toolkit encompasses not just software tools for data analysis, user feedback collection, and project management, but also frameworks and methodologies that guide the ideation, validation, and execution processes. We'll explore how to select and effectively utilize these tools to enhance the product development lifecycle, ensuring our product professionals are well-prepared to translate their visions into reality.

Fostering a Culture of Continuous Improvement

In the fast-paced world of product management, staying ahead means embracing a culture of continuous learning and adaptation. This culture encourages ongoing feedback, both within the product team and from users, to iteratively refine and improve products. It also acknowledges the necessity of keeping abreast of industry trends, technological advancements, and evolving user needs. We will discuss creating mechanisms for continuous feedback, investing in professional development, and encouraging an environment where learning is seen as an integral part of daily work.

Enterprise Support: The Keystone of Empowerment

None of these initiatives can succeed without unwavering support from the enterprise. This support translates into allocating time for learning and experimentation, providing resources for professional development, and recognizing and rewarding innovation and growth. We'll cover strategies for securing this support, demonstrating the ROI of investing in product professionals' growth, and showcasing how empowered product teams can drive significant business outcomes.

What's Next?

"Autonomy Found: Empowering Product Professionals" aims to serve as a comprehensive guide for transforming the potential of product teams into impactful results. By focusing on skill development, equipping teams with the right tools, and fostering a culture of continuous improvement, we pave the way for product professionals to become autonomous leaders of innovation. With the enterprise's support, we can unlock their true potential, ensuring they're not only prepared to navigate the challenges of today but are also primed to shape the future of product development.

Note from Sean:

Warning to all aspiring Product Managers out there, let me be clear: the path to autonomy is not paved with ease. The journey from being a Product Order-Taker, a cog in the Feature Factory, or a pseudo-Project Manager is a steep climb. You're currently engaging in merely a fraction of the work required.

This isn't about taking shortcuts or choosing the path of least resistance. It's about rolling up your sleeves, stepping into the arena, and doing the heavy lifting. Autonomy in product management is earned, not given. It demands a relentless pursuit of excellence, an insatiable curiosity for your customers, and an unwavering commitment to driving value.

If you're content with just scratching the surface, then perhaps this isn't for you. But if you're eager to leave a mark, to be the architect of your product's destiny, and to navigate the complexities of true Product Management, then brace yourself. You're about to embark on a demanding yet immensely rewarding journey. Are you ready to rise to the challenge?

Section 3
Autonomy Found: Empowering Product Professionals

Ch. 33

Defining Product Manager

A Product Manager is a professional tasked with the comprehensive responsibility of ensuring a software product's success. This role transcends mere oversight, embodying the proactive ownership of the product vision, strategic planning, and execution. Central to their duties is the commitment to solving customer problems effectively, driving business value, and maximizing return on investment (ROI).

The Product Manager serves as the linchpin that connects market needs, user feedback, and business objectives with the technological solutions offered by the product, ensuring a harmonious balance that fosters innovation and user satisfaction.

The Archetype of a Product Manager

The path of a Product Manager is pursued by individuals driven by a desire to innovate and solve real-world problems through technology. They are visionaries who not only dream up the next big idea but also possess the grit and determination to see it through to fruition. In the realm of software delivery, this requires a unique blend of technical understanding, market insight, and user empathy. The ideal Product Manager is someone who can navigate the delicate balance of delivering value to users while achieving business goals, all within the constraints and possibilities presented by technology.

Ownership and Measures of Success

Ownership for a Product Manager means more than just shepherding a product through its lifecycle; it's about defining and championing the measures of success for the product. Success in this context is multifaceted, encompassing not only financial performance but also user engagement, market penetration, and the product's impact on solving real user problems. Product Managers are responsible for setting clear, measurable goals that align with the product vision and business strategy. These goals, often articulated through Key Performance Indicators (KPIs), serve as the north star for the development team, guiding decision-making, prioritization, and efforts to iterate and improve the product. Understanding and communicating these measures of success are vital in steering the product toward achieving its full potential in the marketplace.

Stakeholder Welfare and Key Results

The welfare of stakeholders is at the heart of a Product Manager's responsibilities. Stakeholders encompass a broad spectrum, including users, the delivery team, business leaders, and any related products or services. Product Managers must adeptly navigate the diverse interests and objectives of these groups, ensuring that the product not only meets user needs but also addresses core business challenges and opportunities.

This involves working closely with primary stakeholders to define Key Results that align with the overarching business goals. KRs emerge from a collaborative process, where Product Managers play a crucial role in synthesizing insights from stakeholders, market analysis, and user feedback to craft solutions that drive genuine value. By fostering a deep understanding of what success looks like for each stakeholder group, Product Managers ensure that the product's direction and development are firmly rooted in solving actual business problems and contributing to the organization's strategic objectives.

The role of a Product Manager in software delivery is both challenging and rewarding. It requires a person who is not only capable of dreaming big but also getting into the weeds, someone who can lead and listen, and who thrives on making the complex seem simple. Product Managers are the linchpin in the machinery of software development, ensuring that every piece moves in harmony towards the creation of products that delight users and drive business success. This book will explore the myriad facets of this role, offering insights and strategies to navigate its challenges and seize its opportunities.

Role Within a Delivery Team

We discussed previously what the role of the Product Manager is on the Scrum Team as the Captain of the ship. Some of the roles and responsibilities necessary to support delivery are:

- **Backlog Management**: One of the primary responsibilities of a Product Manager is managing the product backlog. This entails prioritizing tasks and features to ensure the team focuses on the most impactful items next. It's a delicate balancing act of aligning business goals with user needs and team capabilities.

- **Eliciting Business Requirements**: Understanding the problem is half the solution. A Product Manager must gather comprehensive business requirements to grasp fully what the team is solving for. This involves deep-dives into the needs and challenges faced by users and translating these insights into actionable items for the team. These are often articulated as:

    - **User Stories**: User stories are short, simple descriptions of a feature from the perspective of the end user. They typically follow a simple template: "As a [type of user], I want [an action] so that [a benefit/a need is fulfilled]." User stories aim to keep the team focused on delivering value to the user.

    - **Acceptance Criteria**: Acceptance criteria are the conditions that a software product must meet to be accepted by a user, a customer, or in the case of system level functionality, the consuming system. They are a set of statements, each with a clear pass/fail result, which specify both functional and non-functional requirements and are used as a basis for the acceptance testing performed by the product team.

- **Participation in Scrum Ceremonies**: The agile framework, particularly Scrum, plays a crucial role in modern product development. As such, the Product Manager is actively involved in all Scrum ceremonies, including sprint planning, daily stand-ups, sprint reviews, and retrospectives. In these meetings, the Product Manager serves as the voice of the customer and the business, ensuring that the team's efforts align with broader objectives and that any feedback is quickly incorporated into the development process.

Ch. 34

Defining NOT Product Manager

What a Product Manager is NOT

We now know what a Product Manager is. It's now crucial to establish what a product manager is not. This clarification is not merely academic but essential for understanding the unique value and responsibilities inherent in the role. A product manager is not simply a manager of the development team, nor are they solely responsible for providing timelines or transcribing business requirements into actionable tasks. Their role cannot be reduced to the conversion of ideas into user stories, although these tasks might intersect with their broader duties.

The realm of a product manager is vast, requiring a blend of technical savvy, market insight, and a profound understanding of user needs. While their responsibilities might overlap with those traditionally associated with roles like Business Analysts, Project Managers, and UX Designers, it's vital to recognize the distinct strategic position a product manager occupies.

Product Managers vs. Project Managers

A Project Manager is a professional tasked with planning, executing, and finalizing projects according to strict deadlines and within budget.

Project managers can come in all varieties, some serve to ensure products stay within established finance budgets (helping with our ROI), some help convey important messages to leadership (so you don't have to) and some are dead-weight barriers to progress. Here are some of the differences between the two positions:

Focus and Scope

- **Product Managers:** Their primary focus is on the "what" and "why" of the product. They define the vision, strategy, and roadmap of a product, focusing on understanding user needs, market trends, and business goals. Product Managers are concerned with what the product should do, why it should do it, and for whom.

- **Project Managers:** Conversely, Project Managers concentrate on the "how" and "when." Their role revolves around executing the plan to deliver the product or features defined by the Product Manager. This includes managing timelines, budgets, resources, and risks associated with the project.

Responsibilities

- **Product Managers:** They are responsible for identifying and prioritizing product features based on user research, competitive analysis, and business strategy. Their responsibilities extend to ensuring the product meets the market needs and achieves the desired user and business outcomes.

- **Project Managers:** Their primary responsibility is to ensure that the project is completed on time, within budget, and to the specified quality. Therefore, they are in charge of scheduling, budgeting, and facilitating communication between stakeholders to ensure project milestones and objectives are met.

Ultimate Goals

- **Product Managers:** The ultimate goal of a Product Manager is to ensure the product's success in the market. This includes driving product adoption, ensuring user satisfaction, and achieving business objectives related to growth, revenue, and market share.

- **Project Managers:** For Project Managers, the goal is to ensure the successful delivery of the project. This means completing the project within the defined scope, time, and budget, regardless of whether the project is a single feature, a product release, or an internal initiative.

Stakeholder Engagement

- **Product Managers:** They act as advocates for the users within the company, often requiring them to balance various stakeholders' needs, including users, sales, marketing, and engineering teams, to align everyone with the product vision.
- **Project Managers:** While they also engage with a variety of stakeholders, their focus is more on managing expectations and communications regarding project status, dependencies, and potential roadblocks.

Skills and Traits

- **Product Managers:** Success in this role requires a strong understanding of the market, user experience, and the ability to make strategic decisions. Creativity, empathy, strategic thinking, and leadership are key traits.
- **Project Managers:** They excel with strong organizational, risk management, and communication skills. A successful Project Manager is detail-oriented, excels in problem-solving, and has strong negotiation skills.

Understanding these distinctions is crucial not only for professionals navigating their career paths but also for organizations structuring their teams to achieve maximum efficiency and impact. While Product Managers and Project Managers work closely together and their roles may sometimes overlap, recognizing the unique contributions of each can lead to more successful product development and project execution.

Product Managers vs. Business Analysts:

A Business Analyst (BA) is a professional who analyzes an organization's business domain (real or hypothetical) and documents its business or processes or systems, assessing the business model or its integration with technology.

BAs can serve a multitude of functions, from documenting and creating process flows to writing advanced SQL queries. They can take a vast load off a Product Managers plate, thank them often. Here are some of the principal differences between BAs and Product Managers

Core Focus and Objectives

- **Product Managers:** The core focus is on the strategic direction of the product. They are responsible for defining the vision, identifying market opportunities, and deciding on the product features that will best serve the users and achieve business goals. The overarching objective is to ensure the product's success in the market, aligning product development with user needs and business strategy.

- **Business Analysts:** Business Analysts primarily concentrate on the analytical and tactical aspects of projects and processes. They define business requirements, analyzing needs, and specifying solutions to business problems. Their objectives often revolve around improving processes, systems, and workflows to enhance efficiency and effectiveness within the organization.

Responsibilities and Tasks

- **Product Managers:** They oversee the product lifecycle from concept to launch and beyond, prioritizing features, defining user stories, and working closely with cross-functional teams to bring the product vision to life. Product Managers also play a key role in product marketing, customer engagement, and feedback gathering.

- **Business Analysts:** Their responsibilities include conducting market analyses, gathering and documenting business requirements, and creating detailed business models. They act as a bridge between the business stakeholders and IT teams, ensuring that technical solutions meet business needs.

Decision-Making and Strategy

- **Product Managers:** A significant part of their role involves making strategic decisions about the product's direction. This requires a balance of intuition, market insight, and data analysis to make choices that will drive the product forward in a competitive landscape.

- **Business Analysts:** While Business Analysts also make important decisions, theirs are more focused on optimizing business processes and systems. They rely heavily on data and detailed analysis to recommend solutions that address specific business challenges.

Stakeholder Engagement

- **Product Managers:** They must align various stakeholders, including customers, executives, marketing, sales, and development teams, around the product vision and roadmap. This requires strong leadership and communication skills to advocate for the product and negotiate priorities.

- **Business Analysts:** Their engagement is primarily with business stakeholders and IT teams to understand requirements and communicate solutions. They need to excel in analytical thinking, problem-solving, and detailing complex information in an accessible way.

Skills and Traits

- **Product Managers:** Successful Product Managers are visionary leaders with a deep understanding of user experience, market dynamics, and business strategy. They are adaptable, creative, and possess the ability to inspire and motivate teams.

- **Business Analysts:** They are analytical, detail-oriented, and have a strong capability in process modeling and requirements analysis. Business Analysts excel in critical thinking, communication, and stakeholder management, with a keen focus on improving business operations.

While there are skills and tasks that Product Managers and Business Analysts may share, such as requirements gathering and stakeholder communication, the essence of their roles within an organization is distinct.

Recognizing and appreciating these differences is crucial for leveraging the unique strengths of each role to achieve seamless product development and business optimization. By understanding the specific contributions of Product Managers and Business Analysts, organizations can more effectively allocate resources and define workflows that capitalize on the expertise of these key professionals.

Product Managers vs. UX Designers:

A UX Designer is a professional who specializes in understanding user behaviors, needs, and motivations through observation techniques, task analysis, and other feedback methodologies.

UX designers are a critical member of the team as they have the power to make the intangible tangible. UX should be involved in requirements gathering from the very beginning.

Focus and Perspective

- **Product Managers:** The Product Manager's focus spans the entirety of the product, from conception through development to market launch and beyond. They are tasked with defining the product vision and strategy, ensuring the product meets business goals while satisfying user needs. Product Managers maintain a broad perspective, balancing user desires, technical feasibility, and business viability.

- **UX Designers:** UX Designers concentrate specifically on the user's interaction with the product. Their goal is to enhance user satisfaction by improving the usability, accessibility, and pleasure provided in the interaction with the product. They deeply understand the users' world, employing design thinking to solve specific user problems and enhance the overall user experience.

Responsibilities

- **Product Managers:** They identify new product opportunities, define the product roadmap, prioritize features, and make trade-off decisions. Product Managers are responsible for the product's success in the market, which includes understanding user needs, setting the direction, and coordinating with cross-functional teams to bring the product to life.

- **UX Designers:** Their responsibilities revolve around user research, creating personas, designing wireframes and prototypes, and conducting usability testing. UX Designers advocate for the end-users, ensuring that the product design is intuitive, accessible, and engaging.

Ultimate Goals

- **Product Managers:** The ultimate goal of a Product Manager is to deliver a product that achieves the business objectives, satisfies customer needs, and secures a competitive position in the market. This often requires making strategic decisions that balance various aspects of product development and market positioning.

- **UX Designers:** For UX Designers, the primary goal is to create a product that offers a seamless and delightful user experience. They aim to solve user problems through design and ensure that every aspect of the user's interaction with the product is considered and optimized.

Skills and Traits

- **Product Managers:** Effective Product Managers possess a mix of business acumen, market insight, strategic thinking, and leadership skills. They must be excellent communicators, able to negotiate and persuade, and adept at decision-making.

- **UX Designers:** Key skills for UX Designers include creativity, empathy, user research, visual design, and prototyping. They must have a keen eye for detail, a deep understanding of human-computer interaction, and the ability to visualize complex processes and solutions.

Collaborative Synergy

Despite these distinctions, the relationship between Product Managers and UX Designers is not siloed but deeply collaborative. Product Managers rely on UX Designers to bring the product vision to life in a way that resonates with users, while UX Designers depend on Product Managers to set the strategic direction that guides their design decisions. Together, they ensure the product not only meets business and market requirements but also delivers a compelling user experience.

Ch. 35

Product Organization Structures

In the realm of product development, the titles of Product Owner and Product Manager often coexist, yet the essence of their roles can vary widely from one organization to another. This diversity reflects the multifaceted nature of product management as a discipline, adapting to the unique needs, culture, and structure of each company.

These choices, in turn, influence how products are conceived, developed, and brought to market. By examining the different models of implementing these roles, we aim to shed light on their potential impact on the product lifecycle, team dynamics, and ultimately, the realization of strategic product goals.

As we explore the nuanced dynamics between Product Owners and Product Managers, it's evident that their roles and responsibilities can manifest in various forms across organizations, each carrying its own set of implications for product development.

The relationship and division of labor between these two roles can significantly impact the effectiveness of the product team and the success of the product itself.

This is Fine: The Guiding Product Manager and Operational Product Owners

In some organizational structures, the Product Manager acts as the strategic captain of the ship, holding the compass that guides the product's direction, vision, and long-term roadmap. Here, Product Owners operate within a more defined scope, focusing on the operational aspects of product development.

They serve as the bridge between the development team and the broader strategic goals outlined by the Product Manager, ensuring that day-to-day activities align with the overarching vision.

However, this division can sometimes limit the autonomy of Product Owners, relegating them to the role of task managers rather than strategic contributors. This offers the Products Owners the opportunity to grow into a more strategic-minded product professional.

Nightmare Scenario: Product Owners/Managers as Conduits with Limited Autonomy

In scenarios where Product Owners primarily function as conduits for the needs of the business, their role is significantly constrained. They relay requirements and feedback from stakeholders to the development team but have limited authority to make strategic decisions or influence the product's direction. This model can lead to frustration on both ends:

Product Owners may feel they lack the power to effect meaningful change, while development teams may feel detached from the strategic vision and business objectives, working in a vacuum of short-term tasks without understanding their impact.

The Ideal Integration: The Strategic and Hands-On Product Manager

It is the option of this Product professional that in the most effective product development environments, the Product Manager transcends traditional boundaries to become both a strategic visionary and an integral part of the agile execution team.

This holistic approach ensures that the product not only aligns with market needs and business objectives but is also executed with precision and agility. Here are some supporting bullet points that outline the characteristics and advantages of this ideal integration:

- **Deep Market Insight:** The Product Manager possesses a thorough understanding of the market, identifying opportunities and threats through continuous research and analysis. This insight informs the strategic direction and innovation within the product roadmap.

- **Visionary Leadership:** They hold a clear and compelling vision for the product, effectively communicating this vision to both the development team and stakeholders, ensuring all efforts are aligned toward a common goal.

- **Active Agile Involvement:** Far from being a distant figure, the Product Manager is actively involved in the agile process, participating in sprint planning, reviews, and retrospectives to ensure the development aligns with the product vision.

- **Empowerment of Teams:** By granting the development team the autonomy to make decisions within the strategic framework, the Product Manager fosters a sense of ownership and accountability, encouraging innovation and problem-solving at all levels.

- **User-Centric Design and Development:** Keeping the user at the forefront, the Product Manager champions user research and usability testing to ensure the product meets and exceeds user expectations.

- **Strategic Roadmap Management:** The roadmap is not just a set of features but a strategic document that balances short-term wins with long-term vision, regularly updated based on feedback, market changes, and technological advancements.

- **Performance Measurement:** Implementing KPIs and aligning with business OKRs, the Product Manager ensures that every feature and product iteration delivers tangible value, contributing to the overall success of the business.

- **Cross-Functional Collaboration:** They facilitate collaboration across different functions, from marketing and sales to customer support, ensuring that the product strategy is coherent across all aspects of the business and leverages diverse insights.

- **Adaptability to Change:** The Product Manager is prepared to pivot the strategy based on new information, competitive pressures, or feedback, maintaining agility while staying course toward the overarching vision.

This ideal scenario represents a blend of strategic acumen and hands-on leadership, ensuring that product development is a cohesive, dynamic process that leads to the creation of products that are not only technically sound but deeply resonant with users and strategically aligned with the business's long-term goals.

Navigating the Spectrum

Across organizations, the delineation between Product Manager and Product Owner roles can fall anywhere on this spectrum. The effectiveness of these configurations largely depends on how well they facilitate a shared understanding of the product vision, empower individuals with the autonomy to make impactful decisions, and ensure alignment between day-to-day activities and strategic objectives.

As the product management field continues to evolve, finding the right balance between strategic oversight and operational involvement becomes crucial. The goal is to create a dynamic where Product Managers and Product Owners (or Product Managers wearing both hats) can thrive, leading to product development processes that are not only efficient and agile but deeply embedded with strategic purpose and user-centric focus.

Ch. 36

Filling Skill Gaps

In my journey, both personally and through the lens of colleagues I deeply trust, we've encountered a recurring theme that underscores a significant gap in the realm of product management today. This gap is not merely a matter of lacking certain skills or knowledge but a deeper, more systemic issue that has been exacerbated by the very dynamics we've dissected throughout this book. It's what I've come to identify as the atrophy of the "problem-solving muscle" in many product managers.

This atrophy isn't due to a lack of effort or desire on the part of product managers but rather a consequence of being sidelined from or not being the driving force behind the problem-solving process.

Look no further than the various product paradigms in this book. When product managers are reduced to mere spectators in the journey of ideation, discovery, and solutioning, they miss out on critical hands-on experiences that are fundamental to honing their craft.

Addressing the Gap: A Multi-Faceted Approach

Deep Discipline Knowledge and Experience

The essence of a truly impactful product manager lies far beyond the superficial tasks often associated with the role. It's not just about translating requirements or filling the shoes of a "product order-taker." Real mastery in product management is born out of an intimate, hands-on engagement with the discipline.

It's about being perpetually curious, always learning, and understanding the subtle intricacies that textbooks and online resources can't fully capture. Everyone who has ever taken the time to read some of the modern Product Management IP will know that some of the practices are extremely aspirational.

This deep dive into the practice—not just the theory—equips product managers with the robust knowledge and experience necessary to navigate the complex landscape of product development.

Problem Solving: A Drive to Overcome Challenges

Central to the role of a product manager is a profound obsession with solving customer problems. This isn't a skill that can be acquired passively; it demands active, practical involvement in problem-solving endeavors. Considerations include:

- Developing a nuanced approach to tackling problems,
- Building a versatile toolkit of methodologies and strategies,
- Ensuring solutions are not just feasible but genuinely innovative and impactful.

Creativity: A Fresh Perspective on Solutions

Creativity in product management is synonymous with the ability to see beyond the immediate, to imagine what could be rather than what is. This creative vision is powered by experience but not limited by the present constraints. It's about challenging the status quo, thinking laterally, and pioneering solutions that might seem unorthodox yet brilliantly effective.

Actionable Step: Encountering Real Problems

The antidote to the atrophy of the problem-solving muscle is clear and straightforward: immerse product managers in real, tangible problems from the get-go. By integrating them into the core of the problem-solving process, they're not just passively absorbing information but actively applying their skills, testing their ideas, and learning from the outcomes. This hands-on engagement is where true learning and growth happen, shifting their role from mere managers to architects of innovative, user-centric solutions.

Ch. 37

Understanding the Customer

Now that we have laid out the steps to build a customer-centric organization, we are now shifting our focus towards empowering Product Managers with the necessary tools and resources. This transition into a customer-focused landscape marks a pivotal chapter in our guide.

Here, we detail actionable steps for both product professionals and leaders, ensuring they are well-equipped to craft solutions that not only meet but exceed customer expectations. This chapter is dedicated to enhancing our understanding and application of customer-centric problem-solving. By bridging the gap between the establishment of a product-centric environment and the hands-on engagement with customer needs, we aim to outline a clear path towards developing solutions that resonate deeply with our users.

It's about moving beyond the foundational principles of customer centricity to actively applying them in the creation of products that our customers will not just use, but love.

The Essential First Step: Direct Customer Engagement

For Product Managers poised to make a substantial impact, the journey begins with a direct dialogue with the users. It's about stepping into the customers' shoes, seeing the world through their eyes, and understanding the nuances of their interactions with your product.

This could involve conducting user interviews, setting up focus groups, or implementing beta testing where feedback can be collected firsthand. An example of effective direct engagement might be shadowing a user as they navigate your application, noting where they hesitate, express confusion, or encounter obstacles. This level of insight is invaluable, offering clear directives for enhancing usability and solving real problems.

Additional Direct Customer Feedback Methods:

- **Customer Surveys**: Distributing questionnaires to users to collect quantitative and qualitative data on their experiences and satisfaction levels.

- **Usability Testing**: Observing users as they interact with the product in a controlled environment to identify usability issues and areas for improvement.

- **Customer Support Interactions**: Engaging with users through support channels can provide invaluable insights into common issues, user expectations, and potential improvements.

- **Social Media Engagement**: Direct conversations with users on social media platforms can offer unfiltered feedback and suggestions for the product.

- **On-site Visits**: Visiting users in their own environments, whether it's their home, office, or another setting, to observe how they use the product in real-world scenarios.

Indirect Insights: The Power of UX Analytics

When direct access to users is limited, UX analytics tools like HotJar or FullStory become indispensable. They offer a behind-the-scenes look at how users truly interact with your product. For instance, heat maps can reveal which areas of your site draw the most attention, while session replays allow you to observe user interactions as if you were looking over their shoulder. A particularly telling feature, "Rage clicks," highlights moments of user frustration—where repeated clicks signal a disconnect between user expectation and experience. These tools not only illuminate areas for improvement but also underscore the importance of designing with the user in mind.

Ongoing Customer Engagement

Regular, direct or indirect engagement with users is essential, not optional. A common misstep among product professionals is believing that understanding of the customer is a one-time achievement, a static insight that once gained, remains relevant indefinitely. This couldn't be further from the truth. The customer-base, customer needs and expectations are constantly in flux, so Engaging with your users should be as routine as any other weekly task, ensuring that our solutions remain as dynamic and responsive as the market itself.

Cultivating Deep Customer Empathy

The ultimate goal of these engagements and analyses is to cultivate deep customer empathy within the Product Manager. Empathy goes beyond understanding; it's about feeling the user's frustrations and aspirations as your own. This emotional connection ensures that every product decision is made with the user's best interest at heart. It's what differentiates a good product from a great one.

Examples and Colorful Insights

Imagine a scenario where, through direct observation, a Product Manager notices that users frequently abandon a transaction process at a specific step. Upon investigation, it's discovered that the terminology used on the button is ambiguous. Simple changes, informed by this direct insight, lead to a significant uptick in completed transactions. Or consider the use of session replays to uncover that users often miss a critical feature simply because it's not prominently displayed. Such discoveries are game-changers, steering product development towards genuine user needs and preferences.

Some Other Tools

In addition to understanding the customer in order to identify pains and gains, here is a few practices that can be incorporated to the discovery process to help Product Managers and Teams be a bit more Customer-Centric.

- **Customer Journey Mapping**: Embark on crafting comprehensive journey maps that chart the entirety of a customer's interaction with your product. This illuminates critical touchpoints, unveiling areas ripe for enhancement and those already delivering satisfaction. It's a strategy that places you squarely in the shoes of your users, ensuring you're not just meeting but anticipating their needs.

- **Empathy Mapping**: Empathy maps are a tool that helps us stand in the user's shoes. This practice sheds light on the customer's thoughts, emotions, observations, and actions. It's a method that enriches your understanding, moving beyond surface-level interactions to grasp the full spectrum of user motivations and challenges.

- **Personas Development**: Forge detailed and data-driven customer personas. This isn't just about sketching out ideal users; it's about breathing life into them with insights gleaned from actual interactions and data. Personas act as constant reminders of who you're serving, guiding every product decision and ensuring they're always made with the user's voice in mind.

The path to exceptional product management is paved with genuine user insights and a deep commitment to customer empathy. By engaging directly with users and leveraging sophisticated UX analytics tools, Product Managers can gain a comprehensive understanding of the user experience. This approach not only enriches the product development process but also aligns it more closely with the users' true needs, ensuring that the final product is not just functional but truly resonant with its intended audience.

In a world where user expectations are constantly evolving, such a user-centric approach is not just beneficial—it's essential.

Ch. 38

Understanding the Product

Armed with the tools to help users achieve their goals and solve their problems, it is imperative that the product manager develops the understanding of the tool to do the job. This may seem very obvious, but as Products grow and change, this fundamental can get away from even the most seasoned product pros.

Refining Product Expertise: The Art of Mastery

A product manager's journey towards mastery involves an intricate understanding of every aspect of their product. It's about being so in tune with the application that they become the go-to source for navigating its complexities.

This expertise is not static; as the product evolves, so too must the product manager's knowledge. Engaging with the product daily is imperative, allowing the product manager to detect nuances, anticipate questions, and provide solutions. This level of proficiency is crucial for writing detailed acceptance criteria that truly reflect user needs and expectations, ensuring that each new feature is a step towards enhanced user satisfaction.

Process Knowledge: Empathy as a Catalyst for Innovation

Equally important is the product manager's understanding of the user's workflow and challenges. This knowledge should extend beyond superficial familiarity, delving into the intricacies of the processes the product seeks to improve. This can vary from product to product in a major way. As product can range from determining the speed of liquid flowing through a mechanical system to ordering a cup of coffee.

This doesn't mean becoming an expert in every technical detail but developing a keen awareness of the user's experience. Such essential understanding allows product managers to identify with the user's frustrations and aspirations, powering a solution-oriented mindset that prioritizes user-centric innovations.

This certainly does not mean that Product Manager are not responsible for any technical know-how. Key areas such as application security, data flow, and the agility of the release process are not just technicalities; they are essential components that impact the overall success of a product.

By developing a foundational understanding in these areas, Product Managers can bridge the gap between product vision and technical execution, ensuring that solutions are not only innovative but also secure, data-driven, and swiftly delivered to the market. This blend of product insight and technical savvy empowers Product Managers to lead their teams toward building more holistic and impactful solutions.

Ch. 39

Technical Savvy

When considering the essence of a Product Manager's role within software delivery, it becomes essential to address the level of technical expertise required. While the position does not necessitate being highly technically skilled, a foundational understanding of technology is paramount. This section explores the balance between technical knowledge and the intrinsic drive to solve problems and enhance user experiences.

Balancing Technical Understanding with Problem-Solving

At its core, the role of a Product Manager is defined by a passion for solving user problems and improving experiences. This unyielding drive to identify pain points, envision solutions, and bring those solutions to life is what sets apart effective Product Managers. However, to navigate the complex landscape of software development successfully, a baseline understanding of the technology underpinning the product is undeniably beneficial.

A Product Manager need not be a former engineer or a tech wizard, but possessing a keen interest in how technology functions and can be applied creatively to solve real-world problems is crucial. This knowledge enables Product Managers to communicate more effectively with their engineering teams, understand the feasibility of proposed features, and anticipate potential technical constraints or opportunities.

Leveraging Technology for Problem-Solving

Understanding technology's potential allows Product Managers to think more expansively about possible solutions. Now more than any other time in history, technology provides new avenues for innovation, making it possible to conceive ideas that leverage the latest intellectual advances to meet user needs in novel ways. This doesn't mean that Product Managers must dive into the minutiae of coding or systems architecture; rather, they should maintain a curiosity about technological trends and developments and understand how these can be harnessed to enrich the product experience.

Bridging the Gap between Users and Engineers

A Product Manager's grasp of technology also plays a vital role in bridging the gap between user needs and engineering solutions. By understanding both the language of the user and the technical team, Product Managers can act as effective translators, ensuring that user requirements are converted into technical specifications that engineers can action. This intermediary role is critical in ensuring that the product developed not only aligns with the technological capabilities of the team but also deeply resonates with and addresses the users' needs.

Data

Product Managers need to have a fundamental understanding of the product data as well as its various sources and repositories. A product manager should be able to draw a basic data flow diagram that can easily demonstrate where data is sourced and how it is leveraged.

Security

Security is one aspect that is often neglected as we rush to build our features, but it is a primary customer concern. While Product Managers might not be security experts, having a foundational understanding of security practices is crucial for overseeing the development of secure applications.

Here's an essential guide to security testing and considerations that should be part of your toolkit:

1. **Static Application Security Testing (SAST):** This technique scrutinizes the application's code (source, byte, or binary) for vulnerabilities like SQL injection and buffer overflows without running the code, identifying potential risks early in the development lifecycle.

2. **Dynamic Application Security Testing (DAST):** Unlike SAST, DAST evaluates the application during runtime, detecting vulnerabilities such as cross-site scripting (XSS) and SQL injection that emerge during operation.

3. **Interactive Application Security Testing (IAST):** IAST merges SAST and DAST advantages by analyzing application behavior in real-time, offering precise vulnerability detection through internal observation.

4. **Software Composition Analysis (SCA):** Given the reliance on open-source and third-party components, SCA tools assess these for known vulnerabilities, ensuring that the application isn't compromised by external dependencies.

5. **Penetration Testing:** This simulated cyber-attack uncovers exploitable vulnerabilities, revealing the application's security posture's strengths and weaknesses.

6. **Security Audit:** A meticulous examination of the application's security measures, from code to infrastructure, ensuring adherence to best practices and identifying potential security gaps.

7. **Configuration and Deployment Review:** This step ensures that the application's deployment settings are secure, involving server, database, and network configurations to minimize vulnerabilities.

8. **Threat Modeling:** A proactive strategy that identifies potential security threats based on the application's architecture, allowing for early mitigation planning.

9. **Fuzz Testing:** By bombarding the application with vast amounts of random data, fuzz testing exposes coding errors and security loopholes that could lead to crashes or vulnerabilities.

10. **API Security Testing:** Essential for safeguarding the increasingly popular APIs, this includes measures for robust authentication, authorization, and data validation against common threats.

Additionally, familiarity with compliance standards such as PCI (Payment Card Information) or PII (Personally Identifiable Information), when relevant, is vital. A basic understanding of these security and compliance standards empowers Product Managers to incorporate secure practices into solutioning, protecting both customers and the enterprise from potential threats and violations.

CI/CD

Continuous Integration/Continuous Deployment (CI/CD) stands at the heart of modern software development, enabling teams to deliver value to users swiftly and reliably. For Product Managers, grasping the fundamentals of CI/CD isn't about mastering the technical specifics but understanding how this practice shapes the flow of value from development to the end user.

Continuous Integration (CI) is the practice of automating the integration of code changes from multiple contributors into a single software project. It's a fundamental DevOps best practice that allows developers to frequently merge code changes into a central repository, where automated builds and tests run. The primary goal of CI is to provide rapid feedback so that if a defect is introduced, it can be identified and corrected as soon as possible.

Continuous Deployment (CD) extends CI by automatically deploying all code changes to a testing or production environment after the build stage. This allows teams to accelerate the feedback loop with customers and reduce the time it takes to release a product.

Understanding CI/CD means recognizing its role in reducing lead times for changes, increasing release frequency, and improving the product's quality and stability. For Product Managers, this knowledge is crucial for several reasons:

- **Speed to Market:** CI/CD enables faster development cycles, pushing features and fixes to users more quickly than traditional software delivery methods.

- **Quality Assurance:** Automated testing in CI/CD pipelines ensures that code is rigorously tested, reducing the risk of bugs or issues affecting the user experience.

- **Feedback Loops:** Continuous deployment means features reach users faster, allowing for real-time user feedback to inform further development.

- **Risk Reduction:** By deploying small changes frequently, CI/CD reduces the risk associated with big-bang releases, making it easier to roll back and fix issues without significant impact on users.

For Product Managers, fostering a deep collaboration with DevOps teams to optimize the CI/CD pipeline is essential. This might involve understanding the tools and technologies used, the stages of the pipeline, and the metrics for measuring its efficiency. It's not about knowing how to configure a pipeline but about ensuring that the process aligns with the product strategy, customer needs, and business goals.

In essence, CI/CD is more than a set of practices—it's a culture of continuous improvement and responsiveness that empowers Product Managers to lead products that truly meet user demands with speed and precision.

Continuous Learning and Collaboration

The technology landscape is ever-evolving, with new tools, platforms, and methodologies emerging regularly. A successful Product Manager embraces this constant change, seeking to continuously expand their technical knowledge through learning and collaboration with their development teams. This approach not only enhances the Product Manager's ability to contribute to discussions on product development but also fosters a culture of mutual respect and shared learning within the team.

In summary, while Product Managers are not required to possess deep technical expertise, an eagerness to understand technology and its applications in solving user problems is invaluable. This blend of problem-solving passion and technological awareness empowers Product Managers to envision innovative solutions, collaborate effectively with engineering teams, and ultimately deliver products that offer meaningful experiences to end-users.

Ch. 40

Industry and Competitive Analysis

Unless the product being produced is completely novel and new to the world, there is probably a crowded industry full of competitors fighting for coveted market share.

It is for this reason that the Product needs to have an understanding of the competitive landscape and how the product fits within it. Who is the leader in the space and how did they get there?

Understanding the Competitive Landscape for Product Managers, an intimate knowledge of the industry's competitive dynamics is indispensable. This involves identifying the market leaders and understanding the strategies that propelled them to the top. It's about mapping out the competitive field to pinpoint where your product stands and identifying the unique value proposition that sets it apart from the rest.

SWOT Analysis: A Strategic Tool SWOT Analysis stands for Strengths, Weaknesses, Opportunities, and Threats. It's a strategic planning tool that helps Product Managers and teams to:

- Identify internal strengths and weaknesses within the product and organizational capabilities.

- Recognize external opportunities for growth and innovation in the market.
- Acknowledge potential threats from competitors and industry changes.

The Value of SWOT Analysis in Competitive Positioning Conducting a SWOT analysis is pivotal for uncovering where your product can shine and where it might need bolstering. It aids in identifying potential areas for innovation and differentiation, enabling Product Managers to make informed decisions about product development, marketing strategies, and resource allocation.

- **Strengths**: Highlight what your product does best, how it outperforms competitors, or any unique resources it can draw upon.
- **Weaknesses**: Acknowledge areas where the product might fall short or aspects that competitors do better.
- **Opportunities**: Look for untapped market segments, emerging trends, or customer needs that your product can meet more effectively than competitors.
- **Threats**: Be aware of competitive actions, changes in consumer preferences, or industry regulations that could impact your product's success.

By systematically analyzing these elements, Product Managers can craft strategies that leverage strengths, address weaknesses, capitalize on opportunities, and mitigate threats. This comprehensive view of the competitive landscape ensures that product strategies are not only reactive but also proactive, allowing for strategic positioning that maximizes market capitalization and secures a competitive edge.

SWOT Analysis for Dunder-Mifflin Paper

Strengths	Weaknesses
Personalized Customer Service: Strong client relationships due to dedicated sales efforts. **Company Culture:** High employee loyalty and a familial office environment.	**Limited Product Range:** Focus on paper limits market share. **Operational Inefficiencies:** Productivity sometimes hampered by office dynamics.
Opportunities	Threats
Eco-Friendly Products: A chance to capitalize on the growing demand for sustainable office supplies. **Digital Marketplace:** Opportunity to expand reach and sales through online platforms.	**Competition from Larger Chains:** Bigger competitors offering lower prices and a wider range. **Digital Transformation:** The trend towards paperless offices poses a fundamental threat.

Ch. 41

Product Marketing

One commonly overlooked aspect of product management is the breadth of knowledge required to effectively act as the "CEO of the product." This role encompasses far more than just software or product development; it requires a well-rounded understanding of various business functions akin to those a CEO must oversee.

This includes, but is not limited to marketing, finance, the specific domain of the product, and competitive analysis. A proficient Product Manager must navigate these areas with confidence, ensuring that the product not only meets the user's needs but also contributes to the overall financial health and strategic positioning of the company. After all, beyond creating impactful products, a key part of the job is ensuring those products contribute to the company's bottom line and competitive stance in the market.

Marketing

Like it or not, even great products will stay hidden if we do not have a strong marketing strategy to support them. The Product Manager needs to understand the basics of how we communicate the value of our products to our customers. Here are some of the basics

1. **Market Research and Segmentation**: Understanding the target market, including customer needs, pain points, and behaviors. Segmentation should be supported by the development of personas.

2. **Value Proposition and Positioning**: Communicating the unique value the product offers to its users, distinguishing it from competitors. This is crucial for setting the product apart in the marketplace.

3. **Product Messaging and Branding**: Developing the core messages that communicate the product's value proposition clearly and effectively. This includes branding elements that resonate with the target audience.

4. **Pricing Strategy**: Deciding on pricing models and strategies that align with the product's value proposition, market demand, and competitive landscape.

5. **Sales Strategy and Distribution Channels**: Determining the most effective ways to sell the product, whether direct to consumers, through partners, or other channels. This includes defining the sales process and necessary sales support.

6. **Marketing and Promotional Activities**: Planning and executing marketing campaigns to generate awareness, interest, and demand for the product. This covers a range of activities from digital marketing to events.

7. **Customer Support and Success**: Ensuring there are mechanisms in place to support customers post-purchase, fostering satisfaction, loyalty, and advocacy.

8. **Feedback Loop and Continuous Improvement**: Establishing processes to gather customer feedback and monitor market trends for ongoing product optimization.

Go to Market Strategy

A "Go-to-Market" (GTM) strategy for Product Managers encompasses the plan and actions required to successfully launch a product to market and ensure its continued growth and adoption. It details how a product will be delivered to end users,

The king of afterthoughts. One of the biggest killers to a great development teams' effort is the lack of a strong Go-To-Market strategy. A comprehensive GTM strategy is crucial, encompassing everything from the initial introduction of the product to the market, to how customers are supported post-launch.

Generally this is not a burden owned by the Product Manager alone. It necessitates a collaborative effort, usually involving a partnership with the marketing department or a dedicated Product Marketing Manager. Together, they ensure that the product not only reaches its intended audience but also provides the necessary support to foster a positive customer experience from the outset.

Ch. 42

Finance, Budget and ROI

There are some definitions of Product Management that have identified the primary purpose of the Product Manager is 'to maximize ROI.' Now while that is not the stance of this book, there is something to be said about a Product's ability to generate profit. To understand how to solve complex customer problems while also creating monetary value for the enterprise. The Product Manager needs to have a fundamental understanding of a few finance concepts:

RTB and Enhancements budgets

IF you work in a larger, older enterprise you may have seen these two finance paradigms. Although this is something of an antiquated mindset, there are still large enterprises that separate activities of teams into these two buckets:

- RTB (Run the Business) budget encompasses the 'cost' of essential tasks required for the maintenance and support of the current feature set, including bug fixes, troubleshooting, and infrastructure updates. These activities are viewed as necessary expenditures to sustain the application's value, with costs willingly incurred by the business.
- Enhancements budget refer to the 'cost' development of new features, requiring additional staffing and resources. It's crucial to

challenge the notion that enhancements are a cost rather than an investment by establishing financial Key Performance Indicators (KPIs) that highlight the potential cost of inaction and the value brought by new features.

Return on Investment

Return on Investment (ROI) represents the financial gain or loss generated by an investment relative to its cost. In the context of product management, ROI calculation involves assessing the anticipated revenue or value generated by a new feature or product against the expenses incurred during its development.

While pinpointing an exact ROI can be challenging, especially for digital products where indirect benefits might be significant, understanding and communicating ROI is essential for justifying investments in new initiatives.

ROI Considerations in Digital Solutions:

1. **Direct Revenue Impact:** Evaluate how a new feature or product directly contributes to revenue, considering any increases in sales or customer acquisition.

2. **Cost Savings:** Identify any efficiencies or reductions in operational costs resulting from the new development, contributing to the overall ROI.

3. **Customer Lifetime Value:** Consider the long-term value of enhanced customer satisfaction and retention due to product improvements.

4. **Competitive Advantage:** Factor in the value of maintaining or gaining a competitive edge in the market, which can translate into long-term financial benefits.

5. **Brand Equity:** Assess the impact on brand perception and loyalty, which, while harder to quantify, contributes to the product's overall financial success.

By integrating these financial considerations into their decision-making process, Product Managers can more effectively advocate for investments in product development, ensuring that every initiative not only meets customer needs but also contributes positively to the organization's financial health.

Ch. 43

Unearthing Customer Pains and Gains

With a clear understanding of our customer base, the competitive landscape, and the resources at our disposal, it's time to turn our attention to the core of product management: identifying customer problems. This chapter is dedicated to the art and science of product discovery, a crucial process where we peel back the layers to reveal the real challenges and desires of our customers.

Product discovery is not about assuming we already know what our customers need; it's about exploration, asking the right questions, and listening intently to the answers. It's here we learn to differentiate between superficial wants and underlying needs, between fleeting pains and enduring gains. Our goal is to transform these insights into actionable features that not only solve problems but also enhance our users' lives.

We'll explore a variety of tools and techniques that aid in this process, from user interviews and surveys to data analysis and empathy exercises. Each tool has its place, offering unique insights that, when combined, provide a comprehensive understanding of our customers' experiences.

Through real-world examples and practical advice, we'll learn how to navigate the complexities of product discovery. This is where intuition meets data, where creativity meets pragmatism. By the end of this chapter, you'll be equipped with the knowledge and skills needed to unearth the most pressing customer problems and craft solutions that truly resonate.

Love the Problem

Navigating the intricacies of product management, a crucial lesson emerges: the paramount importance of problem identification over solution fixation. As Uri Levine astutely advises, "Fall in Love with the Problem, Not the Solution," this mantra serves as a guiding principle for Product Managers worldwide.

The essence of effective product management lies not within the application's confines but in a profound understanding of the user's challenges and objectives. What are users striving to achieve? What obstacles hinder their progress? Is there a way to remove these barriers or ease their journey? This section details the art of identifying customer problems, emphasizing that the heart of innovation beats strongest when aligned with the user's needs and aspirations.

Root Cause and '5 Whys'

After understanding the value of identifying user problems, the next step is to drill deeper into those problems to find their root causes. The "5 Whys" technique is a powerful method for this purpose. It involves asking "Why?" five times (or as many as needed) to peel away the layers of symptoms and reach the core issue. Here's an example of applying the "5 Whys" to a problem where users are not completing their purchases on an e-commerce platform:

1. **Why are users not completing their purchases?** Because the checkout process is confusing.

2. **Why is the checkout process confusing?** Because too many fields are required.

3. **Why are too many fields required?** Because we haven't optimized our form for user experience.

4. **Why haven't we optimized our form?** Because we've prioritized security over usability.

5. **Why have we prioritized security over usability?** Because we lack a balanced understanding of user needs and security requirements.

This technique helps us uncover that the root cause is a lack of balance between security and usability, highlighting the need for a more user-centric approach to form design.

Value Proposition Canvas (example on next page)

When exploring the landscape of problem identification, there are literally infinitely many methods. However, this book chooses to highlight a personal favorite of the author: the Value Proposition Canvas. This powerful tool is designed to help product teams align their offerings with customer needs and desires, ensuring that every solution is not just a shot in the dark but a targeted effort to deliver real value.

The Value Proposition Canvas is structured around two main components: the Customer Profile and the Value Map. The Customer Profile segment helps teams to develop an understanding of their customers' world, focusing on what they are trying to achieve, the pains they experience in the process, and the gains they seek. Meanwhile, the Value Map allows teams to outline how their products or services aim to alleviate those pains and enhance those gains, creating a clear link between the product's features and the customer's needs.

By bridging the gap between what customers want and what the product offers, the Value Proposition Canvas serves as a foundational tool in the product discovery process. It emphasizes the necessity of falling in love with the problem — understanding it from every angle and dimension — before rushing into solution mode. This method ensures that every product feature is designed with a clear purpose: to make the customer's life easier, better, or more enjoyable.

The Value Proposition Canvas

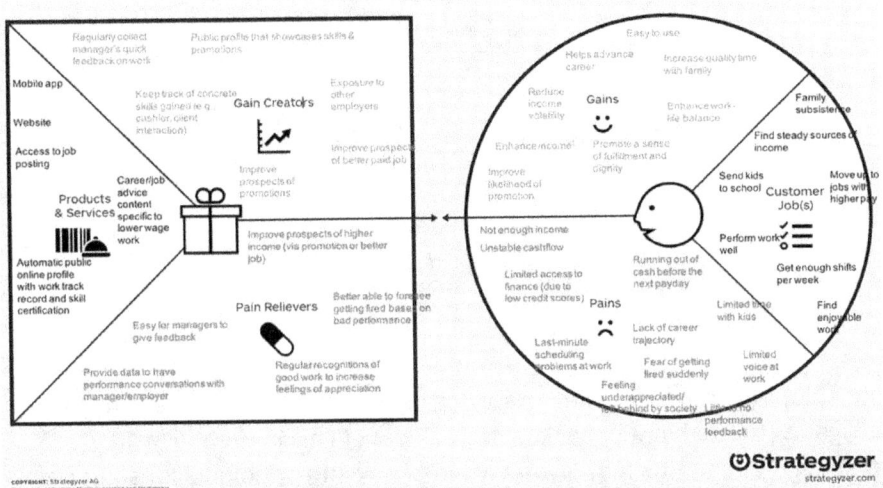

Source: https://medium.com/@dpi662.fall2016/value-proposition-canvas-e747ef3a055d

Ch. 44

Identifying Solutions

Transitioning from identifying to solving user problems introduces us to navigating through critical risks. Marty Cagan, in his influential work "Inspired," delineates four pivotal types of risk and principles for solutioning that every product team must consider. These risks serve as a compass, guiding teams in developing solutions that are not only innovative but also practical and aligned with business objectives. Let's delve deeper into each risk:

1. **Value Risk:** The crux of value risk revolves around the user's acceptance and use of the solution. It's not enough to build something; what's crucial is building something that users find valuable enough to incorporate into their routines. Will the customer find enough value in this solution to choose it over alternatives? This risk emphasizes the importance of understanding user needs deeply and ensuring the solution addresses a genuine problem or desire.

2. **Usability Risk:** This risk tackles the solution's design and its ease of use. A solution could theoretically provide immense value, but if users struggle to navigate or understand it, its potential remains untapped. Can users intuitively figure out how to use the product to achieve their goals? Usability risk underscores the necessity of a user-centric design approach that prioritizes clarity, simplicity, and intuitiveness.

3. **Feasibility Risk:** Feasibility addresses the team's capability to bring the envisioned solution to life within the constraints of technology,

time, and resources. It asks, "Given our current technology stack, expertise, and timeframe, can we build this solution?" This risk necessitates close collaboration between product managers, designers, and engineers to ensure the proposed solution is technically achievable and can be developed with the available resources.

4. **Business Viability Risk:** Even if a solution is valuable to the user, usable, and technically feasible, it must also align with the business's goals and model. This risk evaluates whether the solution contributes to the business's overarching objectives, such as revenue growth, customer satisfaction, or market expansion. Does this solution fit within our business model, and will it contribute to our strategic goals? Understanding business viability involves analyzing market trends, competitive landscape, and the financial implications of the proposed solution.

The Birth of Autonomy

Building on the foundation laid by identifying and understanding user problems, as well as assessing the critical risks outlined by Marty Cagan, it's crucial to highlight the principles that drive effective problem-solving within product teams. Central to these principles is the belief that the responsibility for deciding what gets built rests squarely with the Product Team. This approach emphasizes the importance of not having solutions predetermined by the business, as such prescriptions often impose unnecessary constraints on the discovery process.

Remember, there are fundamentally two approaches to marketing: providing customers with what they articulate as their needs, and delivering innovative solutions to needs they hadn't even realized they had. The latter is where true product differentiation and competitive advantage lie. To achieve this level of autonomy and innovation, the Product Team must be empowered to lead the charge in solving problems and proposing solutions.

It's important to note the use of the term "Product Team" rather than solely "Product Manager." This distinction underscores that the responsibility for identifying and implementing solutions does not fall on the Product Manager alone. In practice, the most successful Product Teams engage in a collaborative effort, leveraging the collective expertise and creativity of the entire team. This collaboration often involves the Product Manager working closely with developers, designers, and other stakeholders to explore the realm of what's possible within the system's capabilities and constraints.

Alignment With Business Goals

Having pinpointed user problems and recognized the collective responsibility within the Product Team to devise solutions, the next crucial step is aligning these efforts with the overarching business objectives. This alignment ensures that the problems being tackled are not only relevant to the user but also contribute significantly to the enterprise's strategic goals.

Here, the concept of Objectives and Key Results (OKRs) introduced earlier becomes pivotal. In a truly Product-Centric Organization, OKRs define the highest-value business outcomes agreed upon by all stakeholders. By aligning problem-solving efforts with these OKRs, the Product Team ensures that their work directly contributes to achieving key business milestones.

Setting Clear Key Results

The journey from identifying a problem to implementing a solution requires clear benchmarks to validate the hypothesis that the proposed solution will not only ameliorate the user's condition but will also have a positive impact on the business. Establishing Key Results for each problem-solving initiative provides these benchmarks. These Key Results should be specific, measurable outcomes that signify success.

Alongside Key Results, defining Key Performance Indicators (KPIs) for each solution implemented allows for ongoing measurement of its effectiveness and its contribution towards the overarching business goals. This structured approach to aligning product development efforts with business objectives ensures that every feature, every update, and every new direction not only serves the user but also propels the business forward in a meaningful way.

Ch. 45

Embracing Continuous Improvement

Live the Change for Product

Embracing Continuous Evolution: The realm of Product Management, much like the technology it seeks to harness, is perpetually evolving. It demands of us a commitment not just to adapt but to anticipate and shape the future of how products enrich lives. This continuous evolution isn't optional—it's essential for delivering value that resonates deeply with our customers and stays ahead of the curve.

Continuous Improvement: At the heart of sustaining this dynamic discipline is the principle of continuous improvement. It compels us to regularly scrutinize our methodologies, seeking not just to identify shortcomings but to uncover opportunities for refinement and innovation. This involves engaging in reflective practices such as retrospectives, which scrutinize our processes, deliveries, and solutions to distill actionable insights.

Staying Informed and Engaged: Keeping pace with the product management field necessitates an investment in learning and development. This means seeking out resources, embracing coaching, and pursuing certification programs that propel the discipline forward. We should immerse ourselves in the wisdom shared at leading product conferences and digest the insights of industry pioneers. This commitment to learning keeps us agile, informed, and ready to lead with vision.

Learning from Failure: Honesty about our missteps paves the way for transformative growth. The path of product innovation is strewn with challenges, and it's our response to these setbacks that defines our journey. Each failure, when leveraged as a learning opportunity, becomes a steppingstone towards excellence.

Fostering a Culture of Innovation: Encourage your teams to venture beyond the familiar. Innovation thrives in environments where questioning the status quo is not just tolerated but celebrated. While we advocate for a disciplined approach to validation, it's crucial to support those who dare to dream big. Remember, without risk, the reward remains elusive.

Resources for the Aspiring Product Professional: For a deeper dive into the intricacies of product management, Marty Cagan's series on product organizations and leadership offers an unparalleled roadmap. Tony Fadell's "Build" not only enriches your knowledge base but connects you to a community of like-minded professionals, all committed to crafting exceptional products.

The Journey Ahead: Embrace this journey with all its twists and turns. Commit wholeheartedly, and even in moments of stumble, know that each step brings you closer to realizing your product potential. Continuous improvement isn't just a strategy; it's a mindset that ensures your work, your team, and your products continually resonate with excellence and innovation.

Ch. 46

The Path Forward

Quick Re-cap

As we approach the conclusion of our exploration into the multifaceted world of product management, it's imperative to reflect on the journey we've undertaken together. From dissecting the oft-romanticized vision of product management to confronting the harsh realities many product professionals face daily, this book has sought to peel back the layers of a complex discipline mired in both challenges and opportunities.

We began by dismantling the myths that surround the product management role, revealing the gritty truth behind the dream job. Our journey navigated through the treacherous waters of anti-product environments, where product managers find themselves shackled, serving as mere conduits for others' ideas rather than as the strategic visionaries they are meant to be. We delved into the pitfalls of being a "Product Order-Taker" and the quixotic quest for the "Unicorn Product Manager," examining how unrealistic expectations and flawed interview processes can impede the search for genuine product talent.

Transitioning from identifying the problems to proposing solutions, the second section of our book laid out a blueprint for creating a truly product-centric organization. We discussed the pivotal role of leadership in championing product management, the importance of cultivating a customer-centric culture, and the necessity of aligning product goals with overarching business objectives. By introducing the concept of Product Crusaders, we underscored the need for advocacy within the organization, advocating for continuous dialogue and collaboration among all stakeholders.

The third section of our book, "Autonomy Found: Empowering Product Professionals," serves as a manual for both product managers and organizational leaders aspiring to foster an environment where product autonomy isn't just a buzzword, but a tangible reality. We've shared insights into filling skill gaps, understanding customers deeply, and mastering the product inside out. This section emphasizes the continuous learning process, the critical role of technical savvy, and the strategic importance of industry analysis and competitive positioning.

Lessons Learned

The core lessons from our journey underscore the dynamic, ever-evolving nature of product management. Autonomy, we've learned, is both a privilege and a responsibility. It requires a deep understanding of the customer, a profound knowledge of the product, and an unwavering commitment to navigating through the myriad technical, business, and industry-specific challenges.

We've discovered that the path to empowering product professionals is fraught with obstacles but illuminated by the potential for profound impact and fulfillment. Leadership's role in this journey cannot be overstated—creating a supportive environment where product managers can thrive is indispensable.

Perhaps most importantly, we've learned that the essence of product management lies in its problem-solving core. The most successful product managers are those who fall in love with the problem, not the solution. They are relentless in their quest to understand and empathize with their customers, driven by a desire to deliver solutions that not only meet needs but also exceed expectations.

Future of Product Management
As we stand on the brink of a new era, the discipline of Product Management is evolving at an unprecedented pace. The trajectory of its growth signifies not just an increase in popularity but a deeper, more profound recognition of its integral role in shaping the future of businesses and technologies alike. This burgeoning realization is a clarion call to organizations worldwide:

adapt and embrace the profound capabilities of product management, or risk obsolescence in the face of competitors who do.

At the heart of this evolution is the unwavering focus on the customer. The success of any product, and inherently any business, hinges on the ability to not just meet but anticipate and exceed customer expectations. Product Managers, with their unique vantage point at the intersection of business, technology, and user experience, are ideally positioned to steer this endeavor. Their role transcends mere management; it is about championing the cause of the customer, ensuring their needs and desires are not just heard but acted upon with agility and empathy.

The technological landscape, particularly with the advent and rapid progression of Artificial Intelligence, poses both challenges and opportunities for product management. The dizzying pace of technological advancements demands a product management practice that is dynamic, informed, and forward-thinking. It is no longer sufficient to keep up; Product Managers must anticipate, innovate, and lead. They must be visionaries who can discern the potential of emerging technologies, integrating them into solutions that not just solve existing problems but redefine the possibilities of what products can achieve.

The Journey Ahead

In this context, the future of product management is not just about managing products; it's about leading the charge towards innovation, customer satisfaction, and business growth. It's about creating a culture where every product decision is a stepping stone towards a future where businesses are not just providers but partners in their customers' journeys. As Product Managers, our mission is to navigate this future with foresight, courage, and an unwavering commitment to excellence.

As we look towards the horizon, let us embrace the challenges and opportunities that lie ahead with enthusiasm and resolve. The future of product management is bright, filled with the promise of innovation, transformation, and unprecedented success. Let us ride the wave of change with confidence, ensuring that we, and the organizations we represent, are not just participants but leaders in the unfolding story of the future.

Afterword

As we draw the curtains on this journey, I want to take a moment to step away from the formal discourse and speak directly from the heart. To anyone who has journeyed through the pages of this book, my heartfelt thanks. This work is a testament to my passion for product management—a field that captured my imagination and dedication from the moment I received my first certification back in 2015.

The path hasn't always been clear or easy. Early in my career, I encountered the stark reality that many roles labeled 'product management' fell significantly short of what I envisioned this practice could and should be. Despite these challenges, I've witnessed an encouraging shift towards a genuine appreciation for what a true product organization can achieve. Today, we stand amidst schools, consultancies, and communities united in their mission to elevate product management across the global business landscape. Our collective aim is to empower organizations to not just serve their customers, but to delight them with ingenious solutions to complex challenges.

The realm of technology is in constant flux, presenting endless opportunities for innovation and discovery. As long as there are problems awaiting solutions, there will be product managers ready to rise to the occasion. I firmly believe that product management stands as one of the most exhilarating and rewarding endeavors one can pursue. It's this belief that drives me to champion the cause of genuine product management—beyond mere facilitation and into the heart of strategic problem-solving.

For those interested in continuing the conversation, extending the dialogue, or perhaps challenging some of the ideas presented, I welcome the engagement. You can find me on LinkedIn at https://www.linkedin.com/in/sean-mcauliffe-192712174/ or reach out directly via sean@forefrontproduct.com.

Together, let's continue to push the boundaries of what it means to be in product management, transforming challenges into opportunities and ideas into reality. Here's to the relentless pursuit of innovation, to solving the unsolvable, and to a future where product managers everywhere are empowered to make their indelible mark on the world.

www.ingramcontent.com/pod-product-compliance
Lightning Source LLC
Chambersburg PA
CBHW052159220526
45471CB00004B/1741